English

Language acquisition

**CAPABLE–PROFICIENT/
PHASES 3–6**

Ana de Castro
Zara Kaiserimam

Series editor: Paul Morris

A note about spelling: We have followed IB house style for spelling of certain words, using –ize rather than –ise; and vice versa.

There is a widespread belief that -ize is American English and that British English should use the –ise forms, but for certain verbs/words both endings are correct in British English. The important thing to remember is to be consistent in a piece of writing.

You can find out more information here: http://blog.oxforddictionaries.com/2011/03/ize-or-ise/

A note about command terms: There are five specific command terms for language acquisition – analyse, evaluate, identify, interpret and synthesize. We have emboldened these five command terms in the book, alongside the wider MYP command terms, so that you familiarise yourself with these terms.

Author's dedication

Ana de Castro – I dedicate this book to my grandmother, who introduced me to books and trips to the library at a very young age.

Zara Kaiserimam – To my in-laws, Zarina and Mohammed Kaiserimam, for their boundless enthusiasm and support.

Although every effort has been made to ensure that website addresses are correct at time of going to press, Hodder Education cannot be held responsible for the content of any website mentioned in this book. It is sometimes possible to find a relocated web page by typing in the address of the home page for a website in the URL window of your browser.

Hachette UK's policy is to use papers that are natural, renewable and recyclable products and made from wood grown in sustainable forests. The logging and manufacturing processes are expected to conform to the environmental regulations of the country of origin.

Orders: please contact Bookpoint Ltd, 130 Milton Park, Abingdon, Oxon OX14 4SB. Telephone: (44) 01235 827720. Fax: (44) 01235 400454. Lines are open from 9.00–5.00, Monday to Saturday, with a 24 hour message answering service. You can also order through our website www.hoddereducation.com

© Ana de Castro and Zara Kaiserimam 2017
Revised for the first teaching of MYP Language acquisition 2020
Published by Hodder Education
An Hachette UK Company
Carmelite House, 50 Victoria Embankment, London EC4Y 0DZ

Impression number   5
Year   2025 2024 2023 2022 2021 2020

Cover photo © Goodshoot/Thinkstock/iStockphoto/Getty Images
Illustrations by DC Graphic Design Limited and Oxford Designers & Illustrators
Typeset in Frutiger LT Std 45 Light 11/15pt by DC Graphic Design Limited, Hextable, Kent
Printed in India

A catalogue record for this title is available from the British Library

ISBN 9781471880612

Contents

How to use this book

Welcome to Hodder Education's *MYP by Concept* Series! Each chapter is designed to lead you through an *inquiry* into the concepts of Language acquisition, and how they interact in real-life global contexts.

The *Statement of Inquiry* provides the framework for this inquiry, and the *Inquiry questions* then lead us through the exploration as they are developed through each chapter.

KEY WORDS

Key words are included to give you access to vocabulary for the topic. **Glossary terms** are highlighted and, where applicable, search terms are given to encourage independent learning and research skills.

As you explore, activities suggest ways to learn through *action*.

■ ATL

Activities are designed to develop your *Approaches to Learning* (ATL) skills.

◆ Assessment opportunities in this chapter:

Some activities are *formative* as they allow you to practise certain parts of the MYP Language acquisition *Assessment Objectives*. Other activities can be used by you or your teachers to assess your achievement *summatively* against all parts of an assessment objective.

Each chapter is framed with a *Key concept*, *Related concept* and set in a *Global context*.

Connections   Structure; Empathy   Globalization and sustainability

1 What's in a neighbourhood?

The conventions and **structure** of our different communities **connect** us to the **world**, allowing us to share different interests and values.

CONSIDER THESE QUESTIONS:

Factual: What is a community? What communities are you part of? What is a neighbourhood? What is your neighbourhood called? Where do you live? Who do you live with? What kinds of places are in your neighbourhood?

Conceptual: How many different communities are there in your neighbourhood? Do we belong to just one community? What type of home do you live in?

Debatable: How do the different communities we belong to influence our interests and values? Does your community influence your way of thinking?

Now share and compare your thoughts and ideas with your partner, or with the whole class.

■ What makes a neighbourhood liveable? Every neighbourhood has attractive qualities that draw us in, and other qualities that we may not like as much.

○ IN THIS CHAPTER, WE WILL ...

■ **Find out** about our communities, neighbourhoods and where people live.
■ **Explore** our perceptions of our own communities and compare these with a community in another part of the world.
■ **Take action** to be actively involved and be inspired to create change in our school and communities.

English for the IB MYP 2: *by Concept*

2

Key *Approaches to Learning* skills for MYP Language acquisition are highlighted whenever we encounter them.

Hint

In some of the activities, we provide hints to help you work on the assignment. This also introduces you to the new Hint feature in the on-screen assessment.

ⓘ Definitions are included for important terms and information boxes are included to give background information, more detail and explanation.

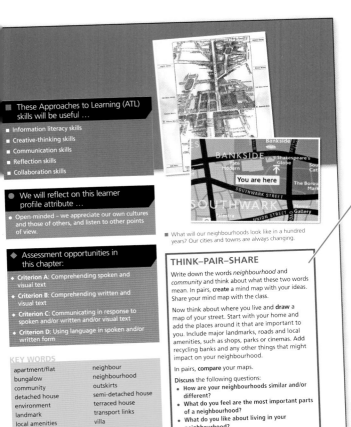

1 What's in a neighbourhood?

These Approaches to Learning (ATL) skills will be useful …

- Information literacy skills
- Creative-thinking skills
- Communication skills
- Reflection skills
- Collaboration skills

● We will reflect on this learner profile attribute …

● Open-minded – we appreciate our own cultures and those of others, and listen to other points of view.

◆ Assessment opportunities in this chapter:

◆ Criterion A: Comprehending spoken and visual text

◆ Criterion B: Comprehending written and visual text

◆ Criterion C: Communicating in response to spoken and/or written and/or visual text

◆ Criterion D: Using language in spoken and/or written form

KEY WORDS

apartment/flat	neighbour
bungalow	neighbourhood
community	outskirts
detached house	semi-detached house
environment	terraced house
landmark	transport links
local amenities	villa
local area	

■ What will our neighbourhoods look like in a hundred years? Our cities and towns are always changing.

THINK–PAIR–SHARE

Write down the words *neighbourhood* and *community* and think about what these two words mean. In pairs, **create** a mind map with your ideas. Share your mind map with the class.

Now think about where you live and **draw** a map of your street. Start with your home and add the places around it that are important to you. Include major landmarks, roads and local amenities, such as shops, parks or cinemas. Add recycling banks and any other things that might impact on your neighbourhood.

In pairs, **compare** your maps.

Discuss the following questions:

- How are your neighbourhoods similar and/or different?
- What do you feel are the most important parts of a neighbourhood?
- What do you like about living in your neighbourhood?

EXTENSION

Extension activities allow you to explore a topic further.

! Take action

! While the book provides opportunities for action and plenty of content to enrich the conceptual relationships, you must be an active part of this process. Guidance is given to help you with your own research, including how to carry out research, guidance on forming your own research question, as well as linking and developing your study of Language acquisition to the global issues in our twenty-first-century world.

▼ Links to:

Like any other subject, Language acquisition is just one part of our bigger picture of the world. Links to other subjects are discussed.

You are prompted to consider your conceptual understanding in a variety of activities throughout each chapter.

We have incorporated Visible Thinking – ideas, framework, protocol and thinking routines – from Project Zero at the Harvard Graduate School of Education into many of our activities.

● We will reflect on this learner profile attribute …

● Each chapter has an *IB learner profile* attribute as its theme, and you are encouraged to reflect on these too.

Finally, at the end of the chapter you are asked to reflect back on what you have learnt with our *Reflection table*, maybe to think of new questions brought to light by your learning.

Use this table to evaluate and reflect on your own learning in this chapter					
Questions we asked	Answers we found	Any further questions now?			
Factual					
Conceptual					
Debatable					
Approaches to learning you used in this chapter	Description – what new skills did you learn?	How well did you master the skills?			
		Novice	Learner	Practitioner	Expert
Learner profile attribute(s)	Reflect on the importance of the attribute for your learning in this chapter.				

① What's in a neighbourhood?

The conventions and **structure** of our different communities **connect** us to the **world**, allowing us to **share different interests and values**.

CONSIDER THESE QUESTIONS:

Factual: What is a community? What communities are you part of? What is a neighbourhood? What is your neighbourhood called? Where do you live? Who do you live with? What kinds of places are in your neighbourhood?

Conceptual: How many different communities are there in your neighbourhood? Do we belong to just one community? What type of home do you live in?

Debatable: How do the different communities we belong to influence our interests and values? Does your community influence your way of thinking?

Now **share and compare** your thoughts and ideas with your partner, or with the whole class.

■ What makes a neighbourhood liveable? Every neighbourhood has attractive qualities that draw us in, and other qualities that we may not like as much.

○ IN THIS CHAPTER, WE WILL …

■ **Find out** about our communities, neighbourhoods and where people live.

■ **Explore** our perceptions of our own communities and compare these with a community in another part of the world.

■ **Take action** to be actively involved and be inspired to create change in our school and communities.

These Approaches to Learning (ATL) skills will be useful …

- Information literacy skills
- Creative-thinking skills
- Communication skills
- Reflection skills
- Collaboration skills

We will reflect on this learner profile attribute …

- Open-minded – we appreciate our own cultures and those of others, and listen to other points of view.

Assessment opportunities in this chapter:

- Criterion A: Listening
- Criterion B: Reading
- Criterion C: Speaking
- Criterion D: Writing

KEY WORDS

apartment/flat	neighbour
bungalow	neighbourhood
community	outskirts
detached house	semi-detached house
environment	terraced house
landmark	transport links
local amenities	villa
local area	

■ What will our neighbourhoods look like in a hundred years? Our cities and towns are always changing.

THINK–PAIR–SHARE

Write down the words *neighbourhood* and *community* and think about what these two words mean. In pairs, **create** a mind map with your ideas. Share your mind map with the class.

Now think about where you live and **draw** a map of your street. Start with your home and add the places around it that are important to you. Include major landmarks, roads and local amenities, such as shops, parks or cinemas. Add recycling banks and any other things that might impact on your neighbourhood.

In pairs, **compare** your maps.

Discuss the following questions:
- **How are your neighbourhoods similar and/or different?**
- **What do you feel are the most important parts of a neighbourhood?**
- **What do you like about living in your neighbourhood?**

What kinds of places are in your neighbourhood?

WHERE DO YOU LIVE?

Community and neighbourhood – what are they and why are they important? Are they just two different words for the same thing? Let's take a look.

A neighbourhood is a place. It is the roads, buildings and green spaces in a local area. People are part of a neighbourhood because that is where they live, physically. A community is a group of people brought together by something that they have in common. This might be where they live or what they believe, value as important or enjoy doing. In other words, people can be brought together as a community by their faith, school, youth club, sports teams or hobbies. Your neighbourhood is your first real contact with the world outside your home. It will influence how you interact with neighbours and with the community that you live in.

Different words are sometimes used to talk about the area you live in. Americans use the word *block* for part of a neighbourhood if you live in a city, or *suburbs* if you live on the outskirts – in other words, an area outside the city. In the United Kingdom, the terms *local area* and *borough* are used to talk about the area in which you live.

Which words are used in your language to say where you live?

Your local area or block is an important part of your community. By taking a closer look at the area you live in, you get to know people in your community and see how it is designed, what it contains and how it has changed over time.

ACTIVITY: Zoom in on your neighbourhood!

■ ATL

- Information literacy skills: Access information to be informed and informed others; Collect, record and verify data
- Creative-thinking skills: Use brainstorming and visual diagrams to generate new ideas and inquiries

Task 1

Visit the website **www.google.co.uk/earth/** and see what you can discover.

Create a detailed map of the area around your school.

Identify the local streets around your school. **Identify** and **label** the buildings and green spaces, and any other places you think are important.

Display all the maps side by side on a bulletin board in your classroom.

In what ways are the maps similar to the map of your neighbourhood? In what ways are they different? Who lives in the area?

Task 2

Now carry out an online search of your neighbourhood or the area of your school. Type in the name of the area near your school and a period of time, for example, Queen's Park in the 1900s. How has the neighbourhood changed?

Write a few **sentences** to **describe** your neighbourhood, to **compare** it as it was then with how it is now. What was it like in the past? How and why has it changed?

Try starting with: The good thing about my neighbourhood is …

Task 3

In pairs, **describe** your neighbourhood. Use sentences from the list below and add three or four sentences of your own.

- There are a lot of green spaces.
- People are kind and friendly.
- There is a large variety of shops.
- The streets are clean.
- There is not a lot of crime.
- The services are very good.
- There are lots of trees.
- There are lots of fun things to do.
- It is a safe area.
- There are lots of very good restaurants.
- The nightlife is fantastic.
- There are no traffic jams.
- There is not much pollution.
- There are public gardens.
- There are sports centres, a swimming-pool and a football pitch.
- Living here is not expensive.
- It is only five minutes by car (on foot/by bus) from the city centre.
- It is multi-cultural.
- There is a lot for young people to do.
- There are a few pedestrian areas.

Task 4

Which places do you like going to in your neighbourhood? Use Google image search or another search engine to find images that show the places you like to go to in your neighbourhood, for example, a local cinema.

In pairs, choose a word or words to complete these sentences:

1. A _____ is a place which keeps people's money.
2. A _____ is a place where you can buy newspapers and sweets.
3. A _____ is a place where people go to learn in a class.
4. A _____ is a place where you can do exercise.
5. A _____ is a place where you go to catch a bus.
6. A _____ is a place where you can borrow books.
7. A _____ is a place where you can see exhibitions.
8. A _____ is a place where you go to send letters and parcels.
9. To catch a train, you go to the _____.
10. A _____ is a place where you can watch films.

Assessment opportunities

- In this activity you have practised skills that are assessed using Criterion D: Writing

▼ Links to: Individuals and societies

Discuss your map from page 4, using the following questions as guidelines:

- What is the name of this place?
- Where is this place and which other places are near it?
- Is it a village, town, suburb or part of a city?
- What types of buildings can we find here and what are they used for?
- Are there any green spaces and what are they used for?
- Who lives here and what do they do?
- Are there any local 'landmarks', that is, special buildings or places?
- What types of transport links can we find?

Find out what the following words mean and use them in your discussion:

- scale
- development.

Vocabulary

Vocabulary is the key to communication. Having a wide vocabulary allows you to develop other skills such as fluency, comprehension and writing ability. Finding different ways to improve your vocabulary has a direct, positive impact on your language skills.

Online tools provide information about words and word meanings. In addition, some tools allow you to practise, review and play games with words.

Digital tools have advantages. For example, many allow you to:

- hear **pronunciation** (the way a word sounds when it is spoken aloud)
- read words in a variety of authentic examples
- view photos and images related to words (important for English language learners)
- reinforce word learning through interactive games
- play with and adapt language
- discover rhyming words
- collaborate with classmates to **create** virtual word walls.

Have a look at these three digital tools to build your vocabulary.

Lingro is a very useful tool. All you have to do is type in a website address on the Lingro website and it instantly turns the website into a clickable dictionary that can translate text into 12 languages. Lingro hides in the background until you need it. To use it, simply click on any word and several definitions of the word are instantly displayed.

Have a go! Go to **http://lingro.com/** and type in **www.layouth.com/seeing-the-potential/** at the top of the page. It will take you to an article called 'Seeing the potential'. This is about a teenager who made a documentary about a South Central neighbourhood in Los Angeles, and how making the film helped him to realize that people can improve their lives. Click on words in the article to see how Lingro works.

Lexipedia is a visual thesaurus that is very simple to use. Just type in any word and Lexipedia instantly displays the target word along with other words. It colour-codes the words by parts of speech, that is, the different words that make the **grammar** structure of a language, for example, **verbs**, **nouns**, **adjectives** and **adverbs**. When you place the pointer over a word, a complete definition is displayed.

Go to **http://lexipedia.com/english/** and type in the following words to see what happens: city, town, house, neighbourhood, community.

Word Hippo is an all-in-one reference tool. It does lots of different things that will help you to build your vocabulary. Go to **www.wordhippo.com/** and **select** words from this chapter to see how it works.

ACTIVITY: Make your own picture dictionary

ATL

- Reflection skills: Develop new skills, techniques and strategies for effective learning

Task 1

In pairs, match the words below to the different features in the picture.
Which of these things can you see near your home?

bicycle stand	crossroad	pavement	traffic light
bus stop	neon light	roundabout	underground station
car park	news stand	signpost	underpass
corner	park	street light	zebra crossing

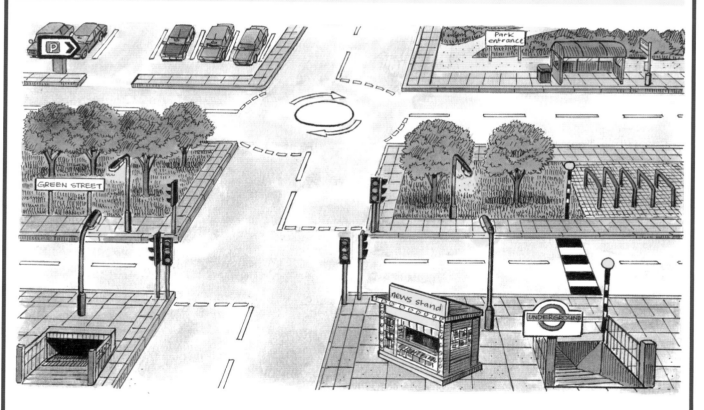

Task 2

Create a picture dictionary that includes images of people and things that you can find in your neighbourhood.

Assessment opportunities

- In this activity you have practised skills that are assessed using Criterion D: Writing

ACTIVITY: My neighbourhood

Read the text below and **identify** the verbs.
The first one has been done for you.

I live at number 10, Harvist Road. I have lots of nice neighbours. They are friendly and helpful. I have two next door neighbours – Mohammed lives at number 8 and Mei lives at number 12.

Every morning, Mei and I leave for school at the same time, and we always catch the bus together. We usually talk about our favourite TV programme, *Teen Wolf!* If I go on holiday with my family, Mohammed feeds my goldfish. Mei has two beautiful cats. When Mei goes away to visit her grandmother, I look after her cats.

The Oliver family live opposite me at number 13. They have two small children and sometimes I babysit for them when they go out.

Mr Gonzalez lives at number 15. He is quite elderly and doesn't go out much. I look after his garden. Mrs Pascal at number 17 is a busy-body! She likes to know everything about everyone – she loves to gossip!

My grandmother lives at number 19. She has lived in the same house for 70 years and she likes to talk about the old days when she was young – she can remember what Harvist Road was like when she was a child. It's a friendly neighbourhood!

Read the text again and focus on the language structure. In pairs, try to complete these rules about the present simple tense:

Rule 1: In the present simple tense, we add _____ to most verbs after he, she and it.

Rule 2: After he, she and it, the verb *have* becomes _____.

Rule 3: After he, she and it, the verb *be* becomes _____.

Rule 4: The negative of *does* is _____.

> **Hint**
> The present simple is used to talk about actions or events that we do every day, things that do not change and things which are always true. To find out more about the present simple go to: http://learnenglishteens.britishcouncil.org/grammar-vocabulary/grammar-videos/present-simple

In pairs, **discuss** what your neighbours are like.

◆ Assessment opportunities

◆ In this activity you have practised skills that are assessed using Criterion B: Reading and Criterion C: Speaking

ACTIVITY: Photo captions

Photographs are often accompanied by a caption that provides more information about the photo and creates reader interest.

Look at the photos on this page. In pairs, write a caption for each photo. You might want to use one of the vocabulary tools mentioned on page 6 to help you.

Would you like to live in any of these places? Can you **explain** why or why not?

What type of home do you live in?

WHO DO YOU LIVE WITH?

What do you see when you look outside your window? Why are homes around the world different? Some homes are large, while others are small. Some homes provide shelter to people for many, many years, while others perhaps for only a few months. Some homes stay fixed in one place forever, while others can move from place to place. There are houses made from wood and stone, and others made from mud or straw. However, they all have one thing in common – they are made for families to live in. We can learn a lot about the way people live through their homes.

The place you live in is your home. The homes in your city, town or village may look different from other homes. Why are homes so different? Well, around the world, places differ from each another and so do people and cultures. Houses are built to suit the needs of the people living in a particular place. For example, the warm brick houses built in England, where the climate is cold for most of the year, wouldn't be suitable for a place like Indonesia where the weather is very hot. Homes have also changed over time because the way we live today is very different from the way our ancestors lived.

We all have our own ideas about what a home is and in this section we will look at what makes a house a home.

ACTIVITY: Who lives in homes like these?

■ ATL

- Communication skills: Organize and depict information logically
- Creative-thinking skills: Consider multiple alternatives, including those that might be unlikely or impossible

Task 1

In pairs, let's find out more about the homes we live in. Interview your partner about their home. You could use the following questions to help you:

- **What type of home do you live in? Is it big or small? What is it made from? Is there anything unusual about it?**
- **Who do you live with? Do you live with your parents, brothers and sisters, grandparents?**
- **What's your favourite room in your home? Is it the kitchen? Or your bedroom? What do you usually do in your favourite room?**

Write down what your partner says and share their answers with your classmates.

Task 2

In pairs or groups of three, look at these pictures of different types of homes. **Discuss** the following questions:

- **Where do you think you might see these homes?**
- **Who do you think lives in them?**
- **Which is your favourite? Why?**

Task 3

Match these words to the pictures below.

bungalow	hut	semi-detached house
chalet	mansion	terraced house
detached house	mobile home	town house
farmhouse	modern villa	wooden cottage

Task 4

Now you are going to **create** your own amazing room! **Draw**, build a model, or make a collage of your ideal, amazing bedroom or special room in your home. Use the words in the box below to help you choose the materials for your room. Use one of the vocabulary websites on page 6 to help you look up or translate words into your language.

Present your room to your classmates. Say why you designed the room that way and what features are important to you. What colour is your room? What materials did you use? What shape is your room?

◆ Assessment opportunities

◆ In this activity you have practised skills that are assessed using Criterion C: Speaking

Materials	fabric	man-made fibres	paper	stone
brick	glass	marble	plastic	wood
cement	leather	metal	polyester	wool
cotton	linen	nylon	silk	

▼ Links to: Design

Construct your dream home

In small groups, collect different materials which can be recycled and that you would usually throw away, for example, tin foil, shoeboxes, yoghurt pots or cardboard. Bring the materials to school and place them in a box. You will also need paper, glue or paste, and marker pens.

Your task is to **construct** a model of your ideal home using the materials you have collected. Think about the shape of your home, and the materials you will use for windows, roofs and doors. **Design** your home and **draw** a floor plan of the rooms.

To help you plan your home, take a virtual tour of a modern house. Go to **www.memorystore.org.uk/gadgets/virtualHouse.html**

Design a neighbourhood

Now **design** your own neighbourhood using the homes you constructed in the previous task. **Identify** other buildings found in a neighbourhood such as a supermarket, bank, police station, church, mosque, school, and so on. **Design** the other elements found in a neighbourhood like the streets, trees and parks, bus stops and traffic. Put them all together to form an 'ideal neighbourhood'.

EXTENSION

Carry out some research about Laurence Stephen Lowry. Lowry was famous for his town and industrial landscapes. Find out why Lowry painted buildings and houses. What colours did he use?

Look at the painting below. **Describe** what you see. Where are the people going? Think about what it must have been like to live in this town? How are towns different today?

■ 'A Manufacturing Town' by L.S. Lowry (1922)

WATCH-THINK-SHARE

■ Communication skills: Write for different purposes; Use intercultural understanding to interpret communication

Task 1

The video '1420 Todd's House' gives an insight into a Japanese style house. Watch the video and listen carefully to how Todd describes his house: **https://vimeo.com/181432477**

As you watch, copy and complete the following sentences:

Todd lives in a _____ neighbourhood. His house is _____ and _____. It has _____ rooms. In Japan, the room you sleep in is called a _____ _____. Before, Todd used to sleep on a bed but now he sleeps on a _____.

The kitchen is _____ and it has a _____, a _____ and a_____. Todd thinks his _____ _____ is cool. It has a _____ TV. There are three _____ in his house. He takes a shower in the _____ _____ bathroom which is _____ the house. Todd thinks his Japanese house is very _____ and he never wants to leave!

Now share your answers with a partner. **Discuss** what you have learnt from the video.

Task 2

In pairs, **select** one of the homes on page 10 and write your own description similar to the one above. Use the example of Todd's house to help you.

◆ Assessment opportunities

◆ In this activity you have practised skills that are assessed using Criterion A: Listening and Criterion D: Writing

What is a multimodal text?

- We don't just use language to communicate ideas; images, whether still or moving, can be combined with text to convey messages or to present arguments.
- Texts which consist of more than one mode, for instance texts which make use of both written and visual modes, are called **multimodal texts**.
- Comic books are a great example of this as they not only use pictures and texts to create narratives, but also include spoken language elements which can make the texts more accessible for readers.
- Can you think of any other types of texts which can be considered multimodal? Use the internet to carry out some research and compile your own list of **multimodal text types**.

ACTIVITY: Big Yellow Taxi

■ ATL

- Creative-thinking skills: Practise visible thinking strategies and techniques; Create original works and ideas; Use existing works and ideas in new ways

HEAR–THINK–WONDER

Listen to the song *Big Yellow Taxi* by Joni Mitchell: www.youtube.com/watch?v=94bdMSCdw20

What do you hear? How does the song make you feel? What does it make you wonder?

Task 1

What is the song *Big Yellow Taxi* about? What concerns do you think Joni Mitchell has?

To better **understand** the song, let's look at the lyrics in more detail. The following is a useful website to refer to: www.songlyrics.com

In pairs, brainstorm ideas or take ideas from the song to write your own lyrics about your town or neighbourhood.

Task 2

Write an **acrostic poem** about your town or neighbourhood.

To **create** an acrostic poem you must write a word or phrase for each letter of the town's name. Look at the example below for the city of Madrid.

Madrid

Always friendly

Day and night

Real Madrid

Interesting museums

Dynamic!

◆ Assessment opportunities

- ◆ In this activity you have practised skills that are assessed using Criterion A: Listening and Criterion D: Writing

▼ Links to: Arts; Language and literature

Artists and writers often use their communities as inspiration for their work. Carry out some research online to find examples of songs or art that talk about neighbourhoods. Note down how they represent towns and communities and their architectural sites through the lyrics or images. What concerns do the artists and writers express through their work?

▼ Links to: Sciences

Did you know that wild animals have homes too, and these are just as different from each other as the homes that humans live in? Some animals build their homes out of mud or sticks, and some live in rock caves. Fish live in water, while birds live above ground in nests in trees. Carry out some research to find out about the different homes of animals.

So far in this chapter we have taken a close look at the neighbourhoods we live in and the different types of homes that people live in. We have learnt how cities are structured in different ways and why understanding our neighbourhoods is important.

What is a community?

WHAT COMMUNITIES ARE YOU PART OF?

What is a community and why is it important? Earlier in the chapter, we identified a *community* as being a group of people who live or come together because of something that they have in common. Communities are important because they allow people to interact and connect with each other, to share experiences, develop relationships, and live and work together. A connected community is a place where everyone feels like they belong. It is a place where people know their neighbours and get involved in local events. If we did not have communities, people would live lonely lives with little or no contact outside their immediate family.

There are many different types of communities. What communities are you part of? You will probably find that you are part of several communities and that one of the communities in which you spend a lot of your time is your school community. School communities support students and improve their well-being.

ACTIVITY: Favourite places

■ ATL

■ Communication skills: Give and receive meaningful feedback

Make a list of your favourite things about your community and write each one on a Post-it note.

In pairs, share your ideas. Write the categories below on a poster. Then stick each of your Post-it notes under the relevant category.

| constructions | monuments | scenery | streets |
| buildings | people | places of worship | |

EXTENSION

Create some images to show your favourite places in your community. Use one of the following methods/mediums to make your images:
- digital camera
- video camera
- photos downloaded from the internet
- paintings or drawings

When you have collected your images, **present** these as an advertisement in the form of a brochure, poster or digital presentation.

At the end of each presentation give each other feedback.

Follow these steps to give meaningful peer feedback:
- Compliment the speakers for their presentation.
- **Identify** three things that you liked about the presentation.
- Make specific suggestions regarding the speaker's use of language and delivery.
- Did they use examples?
- Was the presentation well organized?
- Useful phrases:
  - 'My favourite part was _____ because _____.'
  - 'To improve the presentation, I would suggest _____.'

◆ Assessment opportunities

◆ In this activity you have practised skills that are assessed using Criterion D: Writing

ACTIVITY: A child-led introduction to Shanghai, China

■ ATL

- Creative-thinking skills: Practise visible thinking strategies and techniques
- Communication skills: Take effective notes in class

COLOUR–SYMBOL–IMAGE

Watch this short video of Juewen talking about living in Shanghai: **www.youtube.com/watch?v=ZE-TQKhOdWk**

As you watch, make notes about the things that you find interesting, important or insightful. When you finish, choose the three items that particularly stood out for you.

- **For one of the items, choose a *colour* that you feel best represents or captures its essence.**
- **For another one, choose a *symbol* that you feel best represents or captures its essence.**
- **For the other one, choose an *image* that you feel best represents or captures its essence.**

In pairs or groups, take turns to share the colour, symbol and image that you have chosen. **Explain** why you chose each one.

Task

Watch the video again. As you watch, make notes about what Juewen says it is like to live in one of the world's largest cities.

Consider some of the things about Shanghai that are the same and/or different from your town or city.

Identify the problems of living in a big city.

In pairs, **summarize** the main ideas from the video in a word cloud.

A word cloud is a visual way of displaying words and ideas. You can use a word cloud generator like: **www.wordle.net**

◆ Assessment opportunities

- ◆ In this activity you have practised skills that are assessed using Criterion A: Listening

ACTIVITY: Celebrate a local person

■ ATL

- Communication skills: Write for different purposes
- Information literacy skills: Access information to be informed and inform others
- Collaboration skills: Negotiate effectively

In pairs, use the prompts below to **discuss** and write down reasons why you think local people should be recognized.

- **Someone with a special talent, for example, an artist, musician, sports person or local celebrity**
- **A volunteer, for example, someone who has given up their time to help others or done a lot of work on behalf of a charity**
- **Someone who works to help the community, for example, a police officer, firefighter, religious leader or doctor**

In pairs, make a list of people for each category.

Select two or three people from your list. Carry out some research to find out more information about each person and what they have done for the community.

Use a search engine to look for newspaper articles about the people or interview people who know them. Try to find out as much as you can about what each person has done and the positive impact they have had on the local community.

DISCUSS

For each person you researched, **discuss**:
- **What qualities does the person have?**
- **Which quality do you admire most about the person?**

In your groups, share the information about your chosen people. It must reflect what they have done for the community and who they are.

Think about how you would like to present the information. You could:
- **write a poem about the person**
- **create a portrait gallery**
- **do a role play to show what the person has done for the community.**

◆ Assessment opportunities

- ◆ In this activity you have practised skills that are assessed using Criterion C: Speaking

ACTIVITY: Pompeii – a snapshot in time

■ Communication skills: Read critically and for comprehension; Write for different purposes

Read the text on page 19 and then complete the tasks below.

Task 1

Individually, think about and respond to the following questions:

1 **Where was the city of Pompeii located?**
2 **How many people lived in Pompeii?**
3 **What happened to Pompeii in just one day?**
4 **Identify a word in the first line of paragraph 3 that means the same as 'wealthy and successful'.**
5 **What kind of city was Pompeii before the volcano erupted? Find an example from the text to support your answer.**
6 **What did archaeologists find?**
7 **Why do people still come to visit the city even though no one lives there anymore?**
8 **How do you feel about what happened to the people of Pompeii?**

Task 2

Re-read the text and focus on the language structure. In pairs, **identify** the verbs that are in the past simple tense.

Visit the websites below to find out the rules for the past simple tense.

http://learnenglishteens.britishcouncil.org/grammar-vocabulary/grammar-videos/past-simple-regular-verbs

https://learnenglish.britishcouncil.org/en/english-grammar/verbs/past-tense/past-simple

Look back at page 8 to see the rules for the present simple tense. In pairs, write your own rules for the past simple tense.

Task 3

In groups of three, imagine that your town or city was hidden for 2000 years just like Pompeii was. What evidence, that is, objects or clues, would an archaeologist find that would show what daily life in your community was like?

Write a paragraph to **describe** what your community was like. Remember to use the past simple tense.

■ Items found in the town of Pompeii, Italy, which was destroyed by a volcanic eruption in 79 CE, provide interesting and unexpected insights into Roman life – from diet and healthcare to different neighbourhoods

EXTENSION

In pairs, **discuss**:
• How many communities or social groups can you **identify** in your school?
• **Identify** some of the things that you have in common with people who are part of your school community.
• Why do you need to have a membership to be part of some particular groups?
• **Identify** how your school community is enriched by the different groups that exist.
• Is it possible to belong to several different groups at the same time?

Not very far from Naples a strange city sleeps under the hot Italian sun. It is the city of Pompeii, and there is no other city quite like it in all the world. No one lives in Pompeii but crickets and beetles and lizards, yet every year thousands of people travel from different countries to visit it.

Pompeii is a dead city. No one has lived there for nearly two thousand years – not since the summer of the year AD 79, to be exact.

Until that year Pompeii was a prosperous city of 25 000 people. Nearby was the Bay of Naples, an arm of the blue Mediterranean. Rich men came down from wealthy Rome, 125 miles to the north, to build luxurious seaside villas. Fertile farmland occupied the fields surrounding Pompeii. Just behind the city, was the imposing 4000-foot Mount Vesuvius, a grass-covered slope where the shepherds of Pompeii took their goats to graze. Pompeii was a busy city and a happy one.

It died suddenly, in a terrible rain of fire and ashes.

The tragedy struck on the 24th of August, AD 79. Mount Vesuvius, which had slept quietly for centuries, exploded suddenly and violently. A whole community died on a hot summer afternoon. Tons of hot ashes fell on Pompeii, completely covering and hiding it. It was impossible to see the sun for three days because of the cloud of volcanic ash that filled the sky. And when the eruption ended Pompeii was buried deep. A busy city that disappeared in a single day.

Many years passed and Pompeii was forgotten. Then, 1500 years later, it was discovered again by a team of archaeologists. Under the protecting layer of ashes, the city lay exactly the same. Everything was as it had been the day Vesuvius erupted. There were still loaves of bread in the ovens of the bakeries. In the wine shops, the wine jars were in place, and you could see a stain on one of the counters where a customer must have thrown his glass and ran!

The buildings of Pompeii are still the same as they were two thousand years ago. Inside the houses you can still see the pots, pans and household tools! When you visit Pompeii, all you need is a good imagination to see what life was like at that time!

Adapted from Lost Cities and Vanished Civilizations *by Robert Silverberg*

! Take action: Make your community a better place!

! A big part of being a good citizen is giving something back. You are going to complete a project which means you get involved and give back to your community.

! In groups of three or five, pick something that interests you and something you care about in your community. **Identify** individuals/groups in your local area that need your help. Choose one to focus your project on. How will you help your chosen group? What will your project do? Decide how it will benefit your local or school community.

! One way of documenting your project is to take photos or make a video. You can post your initiative on: **www.challengeday.org/ bethechange/**

SOME SUMMATIVE TASKS TO TRY

Use these tasks to apply and extend your learning in this chapter. These tasks are designed so that you can evaluate your learning at different levels of achievement in the Language acquisition criteria.

THIS TASK CAN BE USED TO EVALUATE YOUR LEARNING IN CRITERION C TO CAPABLE LEVEL

Task 1: Interactive oral – your neighbourhood

- You will engage in a discussion with your teacher about where you live, using the images on this page and the written prompts below.
- The discussion should include a personal response. Try to give examples or **explain** your opinions.
- You are expected to speak for 3–4 minutes.

1 Where do you live?
2 How long have you lived there?
3 Who do you live with?
4 **Describe** your home.
5 Do you like your flat/house?
6 Do you prefer living in a house or a flat?
7 What are the advantages of living in a flat/house?
8 Where do you come from?
9 Do you live in the city or the countryside?
10 What kind of neighbourhood is it?
11 Is it a large city or a small town?
12 Has it changed much over the past few years?
13 Do you like living in your neighbourhood? Why? Why not?
14 Would you recommend your neighbourhood as somewhere to live?

Task 2: Writing task

- Read the writing prompts below and use the images on page 20.
- Write 200–250 words about your neighbourhood using the prompts.
- Do not use translating devices or dictionaries for this task.
- You will have 60 minutes to complete this task.

1 Where you live
2 How long you have lived there
3 Where you lived before (you can make this up)
4 Which neighbourhood you live in
5 The good things about your neighbourhood
6 The bad things about your neighbourhood
7 What you can do in your neighbourhood
8 What your neighbourhood was like 30 years ago

Task 3: A child-led introduction to Hamburg, Germany

- Hamburg is the second largest city in Germany. Visit this website and watch the video: **www.youtube.com/watch?v=tc2NMJZs5Wk**.
- Listen to Zoe discuss the similarities and differences between Hamburg and the town she visited in England with her classmates.
- Then answer the following questions, using your own words as much as possible. The focus is on communicating your understanding rather than on how accurately you use the target language.
- Do not use translating devices or dictionaries for this task.
- You will have 60 minutes to complete this task.

1	What is this text about?	(strand i)
2	**Identify** what type of text it is:	(strand ii)
	■ a blog	
	■ a video	
	■ a website	
3	**Identify** the title of the text.	(strand ii)
4	How long is the text?	(strand ii)
5	Who made the text?	(strand ii)
6	What is the purpose of the text?	(strand i)
7	Where does Zoe live?	(strand ii)
8	What type of community is it?	(strand ii)
9	How old is Zoe?	(strand ii)
10	How is Zoe's home life similar to or different from your own?	(strand iii)
11	Which places would you take a visiting student to see?	(strand iii)
12	Would you like to live in this city? Why? Why not?	(strand iii)
13	Do you like this video? Why? Why not?	(strand iii)

Reflection

In this chapter we have seen how a community **context**, school and neighbours are important to encourage sharing and caring for each other. Community gives people support, a feeling of belonging, and a strong sense of self and **connection** to others. A sense of neighbourhood raises awareness of **globalization and sustainability** issues, and encourages us to develop social skills.

Use this table to reflect on your own learning in this chapter					
Questions we asked	Answers we found	Any further questions now?			
Factual: What is a community? What communities are you part of? What is a neighbourhood? What is your neighbourhood called? Where do you live? Who do you live with? What kinds of places are in your neighbourhood?					
Conceptual: How many different communities are there in your neighbourhood? Do we belong to just one community? What type of home do you live in?					
Debatable: How do the different communities we belong to influence our interests and values? Does your community influence your way of thinking?					
Approaches to learning you used in this chapter	Description – what new skills did you learn?	How well did you master the skills?			
		Novice	Learner	Practitioner	Expert
Information literacy skills					
Creative-thinking skills					
Communication skills					
Reflection skills					
Collaboration skills					
Learner profile attribute(s)	Reflect on the importance of being open-minded for your learning in this chapter.				
Open-minded					

2 How do you pass the time?

Hobbies and leisure activities allow individual **creativity** for **personal and cultural expression** and have a **purpose** to enhance physical and emotional well-being. Talking about our hobbies and interests by making the appropriate **word choices** can help us to connect with others.

CONSIDER THESE QUESTIONS:

Factual: What is a hobby? What hobbies are popular among middle school students?

Conceptual: What is the difference between a hobby and an interest? How can having a hobby improve your personal well-being? What do your interests mean to you?

Debatable: Are hobbies good for you? What do activities and pastimes reveal about a culture?

Now **share and compare** your thoughts and ideas with your partner, or with the whole class.

■ Popular hobbies and interests have changed over time and reflect the trends of how people choose to spend their spare time

○ IN THIS CHAPTER, WE WILL …

■ **Find out** about different hobbies, sports and other leisure activities.

■ **Explore** the relationship between hobbies and personal well-being.

■ **Take action** to review how we include hobbies and interests in our personal profiles which can be a very helpful tool for showcasing who we are, our personality and our future plans.

■ These Approaches to Learning (ATL) skills will be useful …

- Communication skills
- Information literacy skills
- Reflection skills
- Critical-thinking skills
- Organization skills
- Creative-thinking skills
- Collaboration skills

● We will reflect on this learner profile attribute …

- Inquirers – we develop a natural curiosity that allows us to become lifelong learners.

◆ Assessment opportunities in this chapter:

- Criterion A: Listening
- Criterion B: Reading
- Criterion C: Speaking
- Criterion D: Writing

ACTIVITY: Wordscramble challenge!

In groups of three, look at the jumbled up words below and try to guess what each word is.

The words are all linked to the topic of hobbies and interests. Why not time yourselves and see which group can decode all the words first?

ierusel	tipangin
looafltb	angndic
lmteopurc asmge	goya
ivingd	lisnaig
lgtonceilc	

Use a word-unscrambling website like: www.unscramble.com/ to check your answers.

In pairs, think of words for interests and hobbies. Start by making a list in your own language and then use an online tool to help you find the English terms, such as: www.wordreference.com

Use your list of words to **create** a new wordscramble. Go to: www.armoredpenguin.com/wordscramble/

KEY WORDS

free time	pastimes
hobbies	spare time
interests	well-being
leisure	

What is a hobby?

WHAT IS THE DIFFERENCE BETWEEN A HOBBY AND AN INTEREST?

Did you collect things as a child? Stickers, stamps or perhaps something unusual? What are you really good at? The answers to these questions will give clues to the things you like to do in your leisure time. A hobby is any activity that you do for fun. It is something that you like to do in your free time which helps you to relax and connect with other people. If you have an interest in something, however, this means you are curious about a topic or an activity but you do not do it all the time, for example, 'I am interested in poetry!' This can be a little confusing and sometimes the difference between a hobby and an interest can be hard to see.

Of course, everyone is different and your personality influences what sorts of hobbies you like. Perhaps you like spending time with friends, so you choose to play in a sports team. Or perhaps you enjoy spending time at home, in which case you might love to read or look through your collection.

Some people find choosing a hobby an easy process. For others, deciding on what to do can be confusing as there are so many different options. It can be hard to choose what to do. Part of the fun is trying out new things and finding an activity that you love to do!

THINK–PAIR–SHARE

What do you think is the difference between interests, hobbies and leisure activities?

Use an online dictionary to help you.

In pairs, **discuss** your definitions. Do you agree with each other's definitions? Why? Why not?

Share your thoughts with the rest of the class.

ACTIVITY: Do you like/hate/love …?

■ ATL

■ Communication skills: Organize and depict information logically

There are different ways to talk about the activities that we enjoy doing. When we want to say that we like or do not like doing something, we use this pattern:

like/hate/love verb   + ing

For example: Akari **likes** reading. Jacopo **hates** swimming.

Put each of the verbs in the list below into a category of your choice: like, hate or love.

dance	read
draw	ride a bike
go shopping	sleep
listen to music	surf the internet
paint	swim
play computer games	travel
play football	watch TV

Here are some other ways we can talk about the things we like to do:

I'm interested in + verb + ing

I'm keen on + verb + ing

I'm into + verb + ing

I enjoy + verb + ing

For example: I'm keen on reading fantasy books.

Write sentences about your own interests using different sentence structures. In pairs, share your sentences. Do you like and/or dislike similar activities?

◆ Assessment opportunities

◆ In this activity you have practised skills that are assessed using Criterion D: Writing

ACTIVITY: What do you do for fun?

When we talk about hobbies and interests we usually use **adverbs of frequency**, for example, *always* and *sometimes*, to say how often we do things, or how often things happen.

Task 1

Individually, read the texts on pages 30–31 and **identify** the adverbs of frequency.

Task 2

In pairs, look at the adverbs of frequency you have identified. Using a table like the one below, decide where they go, according to how many times you do something – from the most frequent to the least frequent.

To check your answers go to:
http://learnenglishteens.britishcouncil.org/grammar-vocabulary/grammar-videos/adverbs-frequency

Task 3

Look at the texts on pages 30–31 again. In pairs, write questions to ask each person about their hobbies and interests.

Task 4

In pairs, take turns to interview each other about your own hobbies and interests.

Before you interview your partner you need a list of questions that you will ask. Remember that question-word questions are the best type of question to use. Look at the questions below to help you prepare for your interview. Add your own questions to find out about the activities your partner dislikes doing.

● **What are your favourite leisure activities?**
● **How often do you …?**
● **Where do you usually …?**
● **When do you usually …?**
● **Who do you usually … with?**
● **Why do you enjoy …?**
● **Which activities do you not like doing?**
● **Why do you not enjoy these activities?**
● **Which activities do you find boring? Why?**
● **Which new activities would you like to try?**

Try recording your interview on **http://vocaroo.com/** or on a device of your choosing.

In pairs, listen to the recorded interview and give each other feedback.

Task 5

Make a poster about the activities your partner enjoys. Your poster must include:

- **Pictures: You can draw these yourself or find them using the internet.**
- **Text: Write a paragraph of 100–150 words about your partner's hobbies. Remember to use a variety of sentences in your writing and include adjectives to describe the activities. Here are some examples: exciting, boring, interesting, fun, challenging, dangerous.**

Take turns to give each other feedback on the interviews and the poster. Is it a true reflection of what you like doing?

Display your posters in the classroom to show all the hobbies you enjoy doing as a class.

There are three types of questions:
- Yes/no questions: These questions are answered with 'yes' or 'no'. For example, would you like to go scuba diving?
- Either/or questions: You can choose between two answers to these questions. For example, would you like to go to the cinema or the shopping centre?
- Question-word questions: You have to answer these questions by giving more detail and information. The question words are: *what, who, why, where, how, which, whose, whom* and *when.*

EXTENSION

In pairs, carry out some research about hobbies and interests for teenagers in [choose any country].

Use http://popplet.com/ or a similar mind-mapping tool to **present** your information to the class.

◆ Assessment opportunities

- ◆ In this activity you have practised skills that are assessed using Criterion B: Reading, Criterion C: Speaking and Criterion D: Writing

Anjali's hobbies and interests

During the week, Anjali likes to spend her free time at home. She is doing the IB Diploma and she is tired after a week at school. When she comes home, she usually relaxes in front of the TV for an hour. Sometimes, instead of watching TV, she likes to read. She often reads the newspaper and likes the articles on finance and business. Anjali wants to study Economics at university.

Anjali is also very musical. She enjoys playing the cello and plays in the school orchestra. The orchestra usually practise after school on Wednesdays and sometimes at weekends.

Jaheem's hobbies and interests

Jaheem is quite sporty. He loves playing football, and plays for both his school team and a local team. He wants to be a professional football player and dreams of playing for Real Madrid. He is very competitive and gets upset when his team lose a game. The team always train for an hour after school. At the weekends, Jaheem sometimes has to travel to other towns to play games.

Jaheem's other hobbies are painting Warhammers and playing computer games. When he is not playing football, he meets up with his friends and they act out complicated battles. He hardly ever goes out to parties and he does not like studying very much.

Nor's hobbies and interests

In her free time, Nor does not like to stay at home. She prefers to go out with her friends or family. Most weekends, Nor and her friends meet in one of the big shopping centres and go window-shopping. Occasionally they go out to the cinema, but they do not do this often as they cannot agree on the film to watch! Her parents are very strict and she never goes out at night.

Nor loves playing badminton. She plays for the school team and has won local championships. She usually uses her free time at the weekends to study and attend supplementary mathematics classes.

Dawei's hobbies and interests

Dawei is a true scientist! He spends all his free time looking at the starry sky through his telescope. When he is not looking at the sky, he loves to read about astronomy. His room is full of books and posters about the universe. Dawei subscribes to scientific magazines and he has his own blog. He wants to be an astrophysicist.

One of Dawei's other hobbies is playing chess and he loves beating his older brother. He helps to run a lunch-time chess club twice a week at school for younger students. He hates sports and never has time to watch TV.

Nahia's hobbies and interests

Nahia is artistic. In her free time, she enjoys painting, drawing and making sculptures. She prefers to paint landscapes and she is very good at it. Nahia is busy putting a portfolio of her best work together as she wants to study Fine Art at university. She is also interested in photography, and loves to take black and white photos of people.

She likes to hike in the mountains. She always takes a sketchbook in her backpack and gets lots of ideas for her paintings when she is out hiking. Sometimes she goes hiking with her friends and occasionally she goes with her family.

Edvard's hobbies and interests

Edvard is very active and loves the outdoors. He usually cycles to school and only occasionally takes the bus when the weather is bad. He is part of the school athletics team and every afternoon he trains in the local sports centre near his house. He is a track and field athlete and his favourite event is the 100 m sprint. Edvard used to be a keen rower too, but he rarely rows now, as he is training for the athletics regional championships. He wants to do well to get a scholarship to go to university in Canada. Edvard also enjoys watching sport on TV.

Edvard is also interested in comics. He has a large collection. He started collecting comics when he was eight years old. He has some special editions of the Spider Man series.

ACTIVITY: What's grammar?

Grammar is a set of language rules that help you to speak and write in the language you are studying. Different languages have different rules and sometimes it can be difficult to understand all of them, especially in the beginning. Grammar helps you to communicate better and be understood by others.

Look at the previous tasks in this chapter and make notes about the language rules you have practised. Make a list of any grammar areas you feel you need to review or find challenging.

Create a reference sheet for your chosen grammar areas. Decide which sources you are going to use to help you gather the information you need to build your reference material.

Visit this website to see an example: **www.youtube. com/watch?time_continue=2&v=uS0UfFPPTy8**

In groups of three, **create** your own short grammar videos. Go to: **www.powtoon.com/** or use a similar tool to start your own library of grammar videos.

When we think about language and how it works, it helps us to know what the different parts of language are. This understanding makes the rules clearer and will help us become better language users.

Each type of word has a name – these are called the *parts of speech*, in other words, the *group* to which each word belongs. The main parts of speech are:

- Noun: name for a person, place, thing or an idea
- **Pronoun**: word that substitutes a noun
- Verb: expresses an action or state of being
- Adjective: modifies a noun
- **Article**: modifies a noun
- Adverb: modifies a verb, adjective or other adverb
- **Preposition**: word or group of words that joins a noun or pronoun to another word in the sentence
- **Conjunction**: linking word
- **Interjection**: independent word or phrase that express emotion

◆ Assessment opportunities

- In this activity you have practised skills that are assessed using Criterion D: Writing

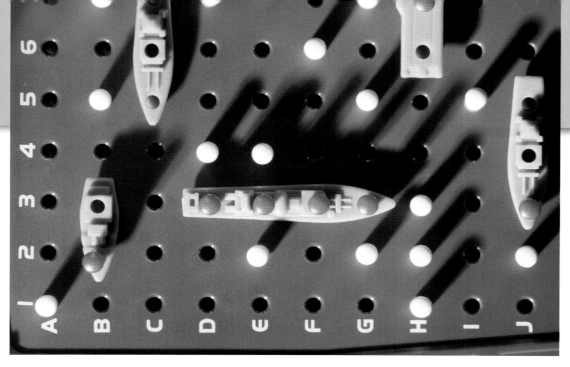

■ Battleships (also known as Battleship or Sea Battle) is a guessing game for two players. It is believed to have become popular during the First World War, when it was known as the Paper and Pencil game.

ACTIVITY: Battleships

■ **ATL**

■ Information literacy skills: Use memory techniques to develop long-term memory

Battleships is a childhood game that many children play at school. The original game is played using a fleet consisting of one aircraft carrier, one battleship, one cruiser, two destroyers and two submarines. It is an easy game to play because all you need are two pieces of paper and a pencil. Nowadays, you can buy electronic versions of the game.

It is easy to play the game using items other than battleships, for example, vocabulary words. Let's have a go using vocabulary on the topic of hobbies and interests from this chapter. Play in pairs and follow these instructions:

1 Before you can play you each need to set up your own board. On a piece of paper, draw a grid with eleven columns down and eleven rows across similar to this:

	1	2	3	4	5	6	7	8	9	10
A					Y	O	G	A		
B										

Along the top row write numbers from 1 to 10, and down the left-hand column write letters from A to J. Your final board should have 100 empty squares on it.

2 Then choose five words linked to the topic of hobbies and interests. Do not share these words with your partner. Write each word on your board – one letter per square. You can write the words horizontally or vertically, but not diagonally.

3 Sit facing your partner, making sure you cannot see each other's board. Take turns to ask questions to find the words, for example, 'Is there anything in square B8?' If there is something in that square, you get a HIT and you can ask your partner what word you found. If there is nothing in the square, you get a MISS and it is your partner's turn to ask.

4 To make it more challenging, when you get a HIT your partner could ask you to spell the word or use it in a sentence.

5 The first person to find all five hidden words is the winner.

◆ Assessment opportunities

◆ In this activity you have practised skills that are assessed using Criterion C: Speaking

ACTIVITY: What's on offer in your community?

ATL

- Communication skills: Write for different purposes

Imagine your school is hosting students from another country on an exchange programme. You have volunteered to have one of the students live in your home during their visit.

Write an email to inform the student about the activities you can do in your spare time in your city or town. Look back at Chapter 1 to review vocabulary on the topic of neighbourhoods and communities.

In your email, include details about:
- **sports and leisure facilities**
- **extra-curricular clubs offered at school.**

Think carefully about the word choices you make.

Remember, it is important to make your work 'look' like an email.

◆ Assessment opportunities

- ◆ In this activity you have practised skills that are assessed using Criterion D: Writing

Writing to inform

To help make your email informative, useful and interesting to read, consider the following features of writing to inform:
- Use a clear, precise and effective opening.
- **Explain** the context.
- Write in the present tense.
- Include relevant detail, such as examples of activities and clubs.
- Use specialized/technical language where appropriate.
- Cover a range of relevant points about the topic, such as times, frequency and cost of clubs.
- Use a coherent, logical structure.
- Write in a style which will interest the reader in the topic.

Writing an email

Writing a good email takes time. First, consider who the reader will be and the purpose of the email. Then **organize** your email into three main parts.

To:

CC:

BCC:

Subject:

- Beginning: Greet the reader and say why you are writing.
- Middle: Give details, but keep it short and to the point.
- End: Sign off politely.

What do your interests mean to you?

WHAT HOBBIES ARE POPULAR AMONG MIDDLE SCHOOL STUDENTS?

We all seem to have so little time to spare. Our lives are filled with school, work and the day-to-day things we need to take care of. School days are getting longer and when most students get home they need to do more studying and homework. So where do we find the time for hobbies?

Middle school students have a lot of options for activities they can do once the school day ends. Many students choose to participate in a sport, watch TV, volunteer, play video games, become members of clubs, and much more.

Some amazing young people not only find time to have a hobby but even turn their hobby into a business! Moziah Bridges is one such student. While his classmates were doing homework and playing sport, he built up his own $150000 business by the age of twelve. When he was nine years old, his grandmother taught him how to sew and he became very good at it. Sewing became his hobby and he started to sew bow ties. He loved wearing his bow ties and people began to comment on them – this is how Moziah's business started.

People who start their own business are known as *entrepreneurs*. In the USA, where Moziah is from, entrepreneurship is encouraged, which is why many young people are interested in turning their hobbies into more than just a pastime. The hobbies people choose are often influenced by the culture of the place where they live. Factors such as how fast or slow the pace of life is, the structure of a town, city or village, and what is on offer locally can all have an impact.

The most important thing is to find a balance between your work and leisure time, and to use the spare time that you do have in the best way possible.

■ How you choose to spend your free time can actually have a big impact on your success at university and later in the professional world

What hobbies are popular in your culture or country of origin? **Discuss** with a partner.

ACTIVITY: From a hobby to a business

■ ATL

- ■ Critical-thinking skills: Consider ideas from multiple perspectives

Watch this video to find out more about Moziah Bridge's incredible story and then answer the questions that follow: www.youtube.com/watch?v=6D5bUoRI720

1 Which IB learner profile attributes does Moziah possess? Give some examples from the video.
2 What does Moziah want to do in the future?
3 Imagine you could meet Moziah. Think of two or three questions you would ask him.
4 What do you think about Moziah's experience?
5 Do you know anyone who has turned their hobby into a business?

Discuss your answers with a partner.

◆ Assessment opportunities

- ◆ In this activity you have practised skills that are assessed using Criterion A: Listening

ACTIVITY: The Mr Men Show

ATL

- Communication skills: Structure information in summaries, essays and reports
- Information literacy skills: Access information to be informed and inform others; Process data and report results

The Mr Men and Little Miss series were created in 1971 by the British author and cartoonist Roger Hargreaves. Roger Hargreaves died in 1988 but his son Adam Hargreaves has continued to create stories in the series. Although many people believe it is a series just for children, the **characters** are popular with a multi-generational audience, that is, people of all ages. Roger Hargreaves used humour, colour, simple images and self-expression to connect with his audience.

Task 1

Visit this website and watch the short video of the Mr Men and Little Misses talking about hobbies: **www.youtube.com/watch?v=GLJpFqYhuuQ**

As you watch and listen, **identify** and **list** the hobbies mentioned in the video.

Discuss these hobbies with a partner or group and decide which ones are the most fun, the least interesting and the most challenging.

Create a word cloud using **www.wordclouds.com** or **www.wordle. net**. You can shape your word cloud to match your chosen hobby and include descriptive words or phrases to go with the hobby or hobbies.

Task 2

A questionnaire is a set of questions created to collect information on a given topic. The questionnaire can be completed individually or as part of an interview.

To find out how to conduct a questionnaire go to: **www.bbc.co.uk/ schools/gcsebitesize/dida/using_ict/questionnairesrev1.shtml**

In pairs or groups of three, **design** a mini questionnaire on how your classmates spend their spare time, the interests they have and how they choose their hobbies.

You can use various sources to help you prepare the questions for your questionnaires. Start by brainstorming questions in your pairs or groups and look at the examples below to help you. Combine the best questions as a class to make a questionnaire.

- **Are you organized?**
- **Are you energetic?**
- **Do you listen to music?**
- **Do you like sports?**
- **Do you like being outdoors?**
- **Are you creative?**
- **Are you a day-time or night-time person?**

Ask other students in your school to complete the questionnaire and collect the information.

Write a paragraph to **synthesize** the results of the questionnaire.

Interpret the data that you have collected on hobbies and interests in your school. Are there any trends? How many clubs and activities are offered in your school as part of the extra-curricular programme? How can you use the information from your questionnaire to make suggestions for new activities in your school?

Summarizing

Summarizing means presenting the main points of a topic in a shortened form.

When you summarize, you leave out many of the details, illustrations and examples that have been given.

To summarize you must **select** the *key* words and facts, and use short sentences.

EXTENSION

Now, on your own, use Google or another search engine to find out about activities and pastimes in different cultures. Search for [name of country] hobbies or leisure. Why not start with your own culture first? Then find out how young people spend their spare time in other parts of the world.

Share your information with a partner or group, and **interpret** and **analyse** the facts together. Can you agree on which activity is the most interesting? Make sure you can **explain** why you like it best.

◆ Assessment opportunities

- ◆ In this activity you have practised skills that are assessed using Criterion A: Listening and Criterion D: Writing

Did you know that writing about your hobbies as part of your personal profile is just as important as listing your achievements or awards? It is important to identify the things you are passionate about and that you do outside school. Listing these activities shows that you have explored a world of subjects, interests, sports and activities which may not be available at school, and that you have been able to develop valuable skills.

ACTIVITY: Building your profile

■ ATL

■ Organization skills: Set goals that are challenging and realistic

Do you know what you like and what you are good at? How can the things you are interested in now influence what you do later in life? Do you ever find it difficult to tell others about your skills when you are under pressure? It happens to a lot of people, especially when filling out application forms and attending interviews. This is why it is a good idea to learn about your skill set.

Create a personal profile with detailed information about you. **List** the things you have already experienced, but remember to list both the things you enjoyed and disliked doing. This is an opportunity to remember, reflect and record.

If you are not sure about what your strengths are or what you have accomplished, ask your family, friends, coaches and teachers to help you. Add to your list anyone who you have looked up to or who has influenced you in a positive way.

Think about the IB learner profile and choose the traits that you think describe you and give examples to support your choice.

In pairs, share your lists of areas of interest and people who are important to you.

DISCUSS

What did this task tell you about yourself? **Identify** the skills that you have developed and how people have helped you to become who you are.

Identify goals that you want to work towards. It might be trying out a new sport or joining a local volunteering group.

◆ Assessment opportunities

◆ In this activity you have practised skills that are assessed using Criterion D: Writing and Criterion C: Speaking

SEE–THINK–WONDER

Watch this short video about a teenager, Sofie Dossi, performing her unusual skill while auditioning for a well-known show, and then answer the questions that follow: www.youtube.com/watch?v=a5P5EyIPBGM

1 Which IB learner profile attributes would you choose to describe Sofie Dossi? **Justify** your answer.
2 How did you feel watching Sophie perform her skill?
3 Why do you think the audience reacts in the way they do?
4 Did you like watching Sophie's performance? Why? Why not?
5 How and when did Sophie start practising this activity?
6 What type of show is Sophie performing in?
7 What other skills do you think Sophie has had to work on to be successful?

We choose to take up hobbies for different reasons – sometimes to relax or to belong. By being a risk-taker and trying lots of different things, we may find something that we really enjoy or something we are really good at. A useful starting point is to consider the hobbies our friends and family enjoy.

So far in this chapter we have learnt that everyone has different hobbies. It can be doing things, making things, collecting things or learning things. In addition, we have learnt to write about and talk about our hobbies and interests with others by making appropriate word choices.

■ By trying an unusual hobby, you might find a passion for something you didn't know existed!

Are hobbies good for you?

HOW CAN HAVING A HOBBY IMPROVE YOUR PERSONAL WELL-BEING?

It seems that many people's only leisure activities these days are watching television and catching up on social media. This is a pity because hobbies, no matter which ones you choose to do, can have real benefits.

Exploring different hobbies, activities and interests not only helps us to interact with others, but is vital for our physical and mental well-being. Our hobbies and interests provide a creative outlet, a context and purpose for personal and cultural expression, and can give us a sense of accomplishment, enjoyment and belonging.

One of the most important aspects of well-being is to *keep learning*. And one of the best ways of doing this is by taking up a new hobby. However, many people are discouraged from doing so because they feel they do not have enough time, or are worried about whether or not they will be *any good* at this new skill.

If you think about your new hobby as something that will enrich you, that is, help you to learn a new skill, you are more likely to enjoy and stick to your chosen activity. Try not to worry about whether or not you are any good at your new hobby, and just focus on having fun. Doing something you enjoy some of the time is better than not doing it at all.

You can choose to do an activity with someone else and this has also been identified as being beneficial for your mental health. Joining a club or group related to your hobby can help you connect with others and feel a sense of community as you work together to achieve something.

■ Taking up a new hobby can be good for your well-being

ACTIVITY: Exploring texts

■ **ATL**

■ Communication skills: Read critically and for comprehension

Read the article on page 42 from an online newspaper about modern-day hobbies.

First reading: Take 5 minutes to quickly read the article and note down three interesting facts that the writer mentions about modern-day hobbies.

Decide what type of text this is:
- **a newspaper article**
- **a descriptive text**
- **a social trend text**

Hint

When you read a text quickly just to get an idea of what it is about, it is called *skimming*.

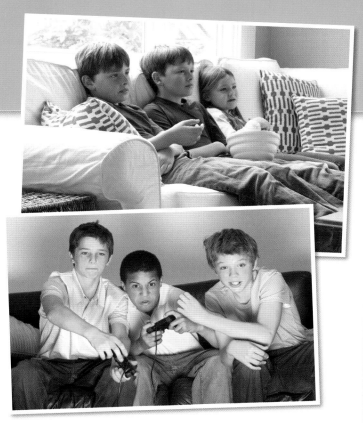

■ 'Healthy hobbies are becoming unpopular, with much of the population now happier to sit back on the couch in front of the box.' – Eleanor Harding, Online Mail

DISCUSS

In pairs, **discuss** the following:
- **On a scale of 1 to 10 how important is your personal well-being to you? (1 = not important; 10 = very important) Justify your answer.**
- **How do you take care of your personal well-being?**
- **What are the dangers of not doing any physical activity?**
- **What are the benefits of doing physical activity?**
- **How can young people be encouraged to take part in a variety of activities?**

Second reading: Read the text again and answer the questions below, referring as closely as possible to the text. **Justify** your answers and give examples when asked.

> **Hint**
>
> When you read a text to find specific information, it is called scanning.

1 **Identify** and **list** the hobbies that are mentioned in the text.
2 Find **synonyms** in the text for the following words and phrases:
   a get healthy
   b hooked
   c abandon
   d have the money to buy something
3 Based on your understanding, say whether the following statements are true or false:
   a Most people have unhappy memories of the hobbies they had as a child.
   b Nowadays people prefer to watch TV instead of practising sports.
   c Fishing is still a very popular hobby.
   d Quite a large number of people enjoy reading in their spare time.
   e Many of the traditional hobbies are expensive to do.
4 Who is the audience of the text, that is, who will read this text?
5 What is the purpose of the text, that is, why has this text been written?
6 Do you agree or disagree with what the writer says about hobbies?
7 Having read the article, do you think people will eventually stop doing traditional hobbies? **Justify** your response with information from the text.

◆ Assessment opportunities

◆ In this activity you have practised skills that are assessed using Criterion B: Reading

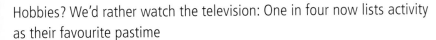

www.dailymail.co.uk/news/index.html

Hobbies? We'd rather watch the television: One in four now lists activity as their favourite pastime

- Only five per cent said they most enjoyed playing a team sport
- Two per cent of the population still enjoy stamp and coin collecting
- A third said they most enjoyed reading in their spare time

Many of us have happy childhood memories of collecting stamps or playing five-a-side football. But according to new research, these healthy hobbies are becoming unpopular, with much of the population now happier to sit back on the couch in front of the box. A quarter of the people now list their favourite pastime as watching television – compared with just five per cent who enjoy playing a team sport.

Only four per cent said they spent their free time practising a musical instrument, while fishing – once enjoyed by many fathers and sons – was only enjoyed by two per cent. Stamp and coin collecting, which had its most popular time in the 1950s, is now only practised by two per cent, while model making has a following of just one per cent.

Campaigners said the failure of these traditional hobbies was the result of a society interested with celebrity and reality TV. Tam Fry, of the National Obesity Forum, said: 'There's a real move now from running around outside to watching TV.

'People have got addicted to reality TV. Television programmes are very watchable and a lot of people enjoy them.

'But it's also easier to watch television. What depresses me is that people say they haven't got time to do other things.

'But if they spent just half an hour less watching television and doing an activity instead it would help them shape up.'

The survey, by Santander, also shows that only eight per cent of people enjoy visiting museums, while nine per cent said they indulged in the arts. Surprisingly, a third of people said they enjoyed reading in their spare time – the most popular hobby of all.

However, in London and Scotland, a higher proportion of people who responded chose TV as their favourite hobby instead of reading. Meanwhile, a fifth chose travel as their hobby of choice and 12 per cent chose clubbing and socialising.

Researchers also found that one in ten people across the UK have had to give up their favourite hobby in the past year because they can no longer afford it. While one in four say doing what they like best with their spare time now costs 25 per cent more than it did 12 months ago. Two in five of those with hobbies say they would like to take up further hobbies if they had the money.

Sean O'Meara, editor of Watchmywallet.co.uk, a money-saving tips website, said: 'It's a shame that traditional hobbies are declining, but it's not surprising. When one considers the cost of most hobbies, compared to the cost of watching television or browsing the Internet, it's easy to see how these activities could replace hobbies when people are looking to while away their free time. Sitting on the sofa is all many people can afford, due to the continually rising cost of living.'

By Eleanor Harding for the Daily Mail, *26 December 2013*

ACTIVITY: Circle of viewpoints

■ ATL

- Creative-thinking skills: Practise visible thinking strategies and techniques
- Collaboration skills: Listen actively to other perspectives and ideas

Task 1

Some of the activities we choose to do help us to develop important 'approaches to learning' skills, for example resilience and patience.

In pairs, look back at the activities, hobbies and interests that you have seen in this chapter so far. Choose ten hobbies and **discuss** the skills that can be learnt from them. Try using some of the 'approaches to learning' words in the box below.

collaboration	organization
communication	perseverance
creativity	reflection
critical thinking	research
innovation	resilience
leadership	self-motivation
mindfulness	time management

Task 2

Consider the viewpoints in these speech bubbles:

Playing basketball is more interesting than swimming.

Watching TV makes people inactive.

Playing video games encourages violent behaviour among teenagers.

Bull running should be banned because it's a dangerous and cruel activity.

Young people find collecting stamps boring.

Students who play computer games perform poorly at school.

Motorcycle racing is a hobby for men, not women.

In pairs, brainstorm some different perspectives to add to the list.

Individually **select** one viewpoint and use the following script guidelines to **explore** your ideas:
- **I am thinking of (the topic).**
- **From the point of view of (viewpoint you have chosen).**
- **I think (describe the topic from your viewpoint).**
- **A question I have from this viewpoint is (ask a question).**

Be an actor – take on a character with your chosen viewpoint.

Prepare your 'viewpoint'. Sit in a circle with the rest of your class . Take turns to go around the circle and act out your various perspectives. You can stand up and use gestures and movement if necessary.

What new ideas do you have about the topic of pastimes that you did not have before? What new questions do you have?

Ways to agree, disagree and partially agree

I think you're right.	That's true, but …
I agree.	I totally disagree. I think …
Absolutely true	
I totally agree.	I feel …
I disagree.	I believe …
I'm not sure I agree with you.	I think it's fair to say …
I don't agree.	In my opinion …
I can't agree with you.	I think that depends on …

◆ Assessment opportunities

◆ In this activity you have practised skills that are assessed using Criterion C: Speaking

DISCUSS

ATL

- Communication skills: Make inferences and draw conclusions

Consider these quotes:

> My personal hobbies are reading, listening to music, and silence. *Edith Sitwell*

> It can be coins or sports or politics or horses or music or faith ... the saddest people I've ever met in life are the ones who don't care deeply about anything at all. Passion and satisfaction go hand in hand, and without them, any happiness is only temporary, because there's nothing to make it last. *Nicholas Sparks*, Dear John

> I don't have time for hobbies. At the end of the day, I treat my job as a hobby. It's something I love doing. *David Beckham*

> I don't really like the word 'hobbies'. *Anthony Horowitz*

What do you think each quote means? Which one do you like the most? How difficult is it to find a hobby? What should you do if you can't find a hobby that you enjoy? Are there any hobbies or sports that people do in your culture that you might not find in other countries?

EXTENSION

Carry out some research on: **What are/were [famous person's name] hobbies and interests?**

◆ Assessment opportunities

- ◆ In this activity you have practised skills that are assessed using Criterion B: Reading

Take action: How can I make a difference?

! Having strong role models, who encourage you to be the best that you can be, can motivate young people to take risks and try out new activities.

! Steve Mesler is a three-time US Olympian and 2010 gold medallist in the four-man bobsled. He is also a consultant and philanthropist who founded the organization Classroom Champions, which aims to address the issue of providing inspiring role models for all young people. The organization uses Olympians and Paralympians as role models for success and goal setting.

! Go to **www.classroomchampions.org/** to find out more about the project.

! Find out which local organization your school can work with. Invite an Olympian and/or Paralympian to give a talk in your school to share their life experiences and the life lessons they have learnt.

▼ Links to: Physical and health education

We have already established that having hobbies and taking part in leisure activities are important. Not only are hobbies fun, but they can refresh the mind and body; and help us to stay healthy, active and happy.

It is important to balance our lives by doing something enjoyable in our spare time, and it is important for the health of our bodies to balance active and passive activities.

In pairs, make a list of at least five activities you might consider doing now or as a future hobby.

Use your PHE lessons to try out new sports.

SOME SUMMATIVE TASKS TO TRY

Use these tasks to apply and extend your learning in this chapter. These tasks are designed so that you can evaluate your learning at different levels of achievement in the Language acquisition criteria.

THIS TASK CAN BE USED TO EVALUATE YOUR LEARNING IN CRITERION A TO CAPABLE LEVEL

Task 1: Olympic glory

■ Visit this website and watch the TED video 'How two decisions led me to Olympic glory' by Steve Mesler:
   http://ed.ted.com/lessons/how-two-decisions-led-me-to-olympic-glory
■ Then answer the following questions, using your own words as much as possible.
■ Do not use translating devices or dictionaries for this task.
■ You will have 60 minutes to complete this task.

1 What does Steve Mesler say about his experience as an athlete? (strand i)
2 What kind of athlete did Mesler's old coach compare him to? (strand i)
3 **Describe** the video using your own words. (strand i)
4 In two sentences, **identify** the type of audio-visual text and its basic purpose. (strand ii)
5 **Explain** in your own words the meaning of the expression 'blink of an eye'. (strand ii)
6 After viewing the video do you think Steve Mesler was right to change his goal? **Justify** your response with information from the text. (strand iii)
7 What are your goals and what can you do to help achieve them? (strand iii)
8 Based on what you have seen and heard in the video, can you think of a time when you changed your mind about something in order to reach a goal? (strand iii)
9 Are you surprised to hear how long it took Steve Mesler to reach his goal? Why? Why not? (strand iii)

English for the IB MYP 2: *by Concept*

THIS TASK CAN BE USED TO EVALUATE YOUR LEARNING IN CRITERION B TO CAPABLE LEVEL

Task 2

- Look at the multimodal text on page 48.
- Then answer the following questions, using your own words as much as possible.
- Refer as closely as possible to the pictures and text, **justifying** your answers and giving examples when asked.
- Do not use translating devices or dictionaries for this task.
- You will have 60 minutes to complete this task.

1 In two sentences, **describe** what the text is about. (strand i)
2 **Describe** the pictures in your own words. (strand i)
3 Why has this text been created? What are some of the features that make you think this (layout, structure, punctuation, choice of words, repetition; diagrams and pictures, graphs, choice of verbs or adjectives)? (strand ii)
4 'This article is targeting a young audience.' Do you agree or disagree with this statement? (strand iii)
5 The text tries to give information about the hobbies of famous scientists in order to make them seem more human. True or false? **Justify** your response with information from the text. (strand i)
6 **Interpret** the message of the text. Do you think it is an important one? Why? (strand iii)
7 Are the scientists good role models? Why do you think that? How do you know? (strand iii)

What Great Scientists Did When They Weren't Doing Great Science

Einstein, Curie, Feynman, Bohr – their names are synonymous with scientific breakthroughs that forever changed our understanding of the universe and ourselves. But even the most brilliant minds need to unwind. Here's how 10 of history's greatest physicists recharged their intellectual batteries.

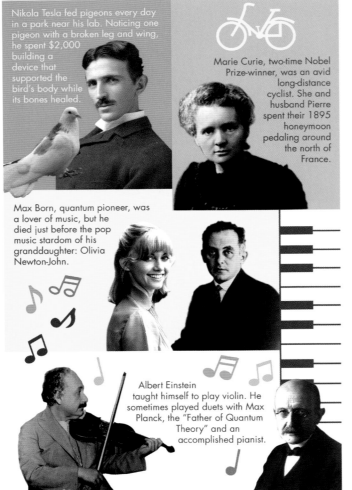

Nikola Tesla fed pigeons every day in a park near his lab. Noticing one pigeon with a broken leg and wing, he spent $2,000 building a device that supported the bird's body while its bones healed.

Marie Curie, two-time Nobel Prize-winner, was an avid long-distance cyclist. She and husband Pierre spent their 1895 honeymoon pedaling around the north of France.

Max Born, quantum pioneer, was a lover of music, but he died just before the pop music stardom of his granddaughter: Olivia Newton-John.

Albert Einstein taught himself to play violin. He sometimes played duets with Max Planck, the "Father of Quantum Theory" and an accomplished pianist.

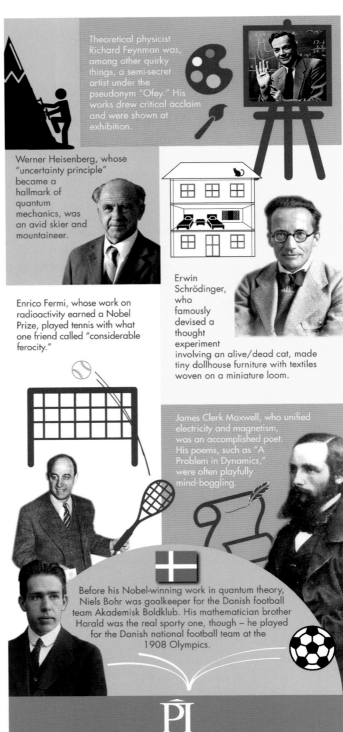

Theoretical physicist Richard Feynman was, among other quirky things, a semi-secret artist under the pseudonym "Ofey." His works drew critical acclaim and were shown at exhibition.

Werner Heisenberg, whose "uncertainty principle" became a hallmark of quantum mechanics, was an avid skier and mountaineer.

Enrico Fermi, whose work on radioactivity earned a Nobel Prize, played tennis with what one friend called "considerable ferocity."

Erwin Schrödinger, who famously devised a thought experiment involving an alive/dead cat, made tiny dollhouse furniture with textiles woven on a miniature loom.

James Clerk Maxwell, who unified electricity and magnetism, was an accomplished poet. His poems, such as "A Problem in Dynamics," were often playfully mind-boggling.

Before his Nobel-winning work in quantum theory, Niels Bohr was goalkeeper for the Danish football team Akademisk Boldklub. His mathematician brother Harald was the real sporty one, though – he played for the Danish national football team at the 1908 Olympics.

PI
PERIMETER INSTITUTE

Reflection

In this chapter we have learnt what hobbies are and the purpose they fulfil. We have seen how, outside of school and work, many people enjoy spending their free time on recreational activities and how these interests can be a form of **personal and cultural expression**. We have also explored how hobbies can be a way to develop and express our **creativity**, relieve stress and even improve our physical well-being. In addition, we have learnt to talk about our hobbies and interests with others by making the appropriate **word choices**.

Use this table to reflect on your own learning in this chapter					
Questions we asked	Answers we found	Any further questions now?			
Factual: What is a hobby? What hobbies are popular among middle school students?					
Conceptual: What is the difference between a hobby and an interest? How can having a hobby improve your personal well-being? What do your interests mean to you?					
Debatable: Are hobbies good for you? What do activities and pastimes reveal about a culture?					
Approaches to learning you used in this chapter	Description – what new skills did you learn?	How well did you master the skills?			
		Novice	Learner	Practitioner	Expert
Communication skills					
Information literacy skills					
Reflection skills					
Critical-thinking skills					
Organization skills					
Creative-thinking skills					
Collaboration skills					
Learner profile attribute(s)	Reflect on the importance of being a good inquirer for your learning in this chapter.				
Inquirers					

3 In a world where there are 6500 languages, how can we understand each other?

Being able to speak more than one language allows us to **communicate** a familiar **message** in a new way and can give us the means to develop **relationships** with others as well as preserve our individual and collective **identities**.

CONSIDER THESE QUESTIONS:

Factual: What is language? How many languages can you speak? What is your 'mother tongue'?

Conceptual: What advantages are there to being able to speak more than one language?

Debatable: Should we learn to speak new languages? Should English be the universal language?

Now **share and compare** your thoughts and ideas with your partner, or with the whole class.

■ It's good to talk! A group of teenagers enjoy a chat over coffee.

○ IN THIS CHAPTER, WE WILL …

■ **Find out** more about the languages spoken worldwide.
■ **Explore** the advantages of being plurilingual.
■ **Take action** to help foster a language-learning culture in our school and celebrate linguistic diversity.

These Approaches to Learning (ATL) skills will be useful ...

- Collaboration skills
- Communication skills
- Information literacy skills
- Reflection skills
- Media literacy skills
- Transfer skills

We will reflect on this learner profile attribute ...

- Communicators – we express ourselves confidently and creatively in more than one language and in many ways. We collaborate effectively, listening carefully to the perspectives of other individuals and groups.

Assessment opportunities in this chapter:

- Criterion A: Listening
- Criterion B: Reading
- Criterion C: Speaking
- Criterion D: Writing

■ How many languages can you speak?

ACTIVITY: Idiom Dingbats

Dingbats is a popular game in which players have to identify a word or well-known saying from a series of images or symbols.

In pairs, remind yourselves of what an **idiom** is. If you get stuck, use Google or another search engine to help you.

Now see if you can **identify** the five idioms formed by reading across the pairs of images below.

DISCUSS

What is your first language? Can you speak any other languages?

KEY WORDS

bilingual	polyglot
monolingual	script
mother tongue	universal language
plurilingual	

What is language?

HOW MANY LANGUAGES CAN YOU SPEAK?

Language can be defined as a system of communication which we, as humans, use to exchange ideas and opinions, feelings and beliefs. Language consists of individual words which are combined in a structured way to produce sentences.

Without language we would be lost. Humans thrive on interacting with one another and much of our success as a species is due to our advanced means of communication. Language allows us to transmit knowledge and information, assert our individual and cultural identities and, most importantly, build relationships with those around us – both locally and globally.

Today, approximately 6500 languages are spoken worldwide! With all these different languages, it seems remarkable that we function so well as a global community. The secret lies in our ability to learn new languages with relative ease. Most languages share a similar grammatical structure, but some languages are easier for some nationalities to learn than others. This is especially true for languages which share a root language – the language from which they originate. Let's take Spanish and Italian for example. Both of these languages come from Latin, so Spanish speakers can pick up Italian more easily than say a language like Urdu, which has different roots.

People who are able to speak two languages fluently are *bilingual*. *Plurilingualism* is the use of two or more languages, either by an individual or a community.

In this chapter we will explore the many benefits of speaking another language.

■ Being able to speak more than one language can help us connect with others

THINK–PAIR–SHARE

■ **ATL**

■ Collaboration skills: Listen actively to other perspectives and ideas

On your own, think about the following questions:
- **How many languages do you speak?**
- **What do you think the advantages are of speaking more than one language?**
- **What challenges do you face as a bilingual/plurilingual person?**
- **Which language is your dominant language?**
- **Which language do you think in?**
- **Which language do you dream in?**

Share your answers with a partner. Are your experiences similar to those of others?

◆ **Assessment opportunities**

◆ In this activity you have practised skills that are assessed using Criterion C: Speaking

Did you know that …

- around 75 per cent of the world's population do not speak any English
- Mandarin Chinese is the most spoken language in the world
- there are about 2200 languages in Asia alone
- there are around 2400 languages which are in danger of becoming extinct. We have already lost 231 languages. It is not just plants or animals that can be endangered!

ACTIVITY: Banana, banana?

■ ATL

- Communication skills: Interpret and use effectively modes of non-verbal communication

Is it possible to communicate with others if we don't share the same language? Let's find out.

In pairs or groups of three, **select** *one* of the following scenarios, but do not tell the rest of your class which one you have chosen:

- **A teenager is looking for her headphones in her bedroom but cannot find them. She goes into her younger brother's bedroom to ask him if he has seen them and finds him using them. She is angry and they argue.**
- **Two parents are waiting for their teenager to come home. The teenager is very late and the parents are anxious. Eventually the teenager arrives home but is not at all apologetic. The parents get angry and the teenager responds similarly.**
- **A teenage boy is happily waiting for his girlfriend to arrive at a coffee shop. She arrives, but plans to break up with him. She does not want to be unkind, but needs to be clear. He does not suspect a thing.**

Act out your chosen scenario in front of your class – but there is a catch. You can only say the word *banana*! The rest of the class must guess what is going on. Ask your classmates to **explain** how they worked out what was happening without understanding what you were saying.

This activity shows us that although language is important, we can communicate in other ways. We can show our emotions through laughter and tears, we can use facial expressions and gestures to get our points across, and we can raise or lower the volume of our voice to express our moods and feelings.

Can you think of a scenario where you have managed to communicate with someone successfully without sharing a language? Perhaps you were on holiday in a place where you did not speak the local language. **Discuss** your experience with a partner or group.

◆ Assessment opportunities

◆ In this activity you have practised skills that are assessed using Criterion C: Speaking

ACTIVITY: Language project

Is there a particular language that you have always liked the sound of? A language that maybe you would like to learn one day? Or perhaps there is a place or culture associated with a particular language that you are interested in learning more about?

Well, here's your chance to carry out some research on a language of your choice.

Before you begin, in pairs or groups of three, **create** a mind map of the languages you might like to **explore**. Share ideas and make sure you can **justify** your choices.

Choose a language, any language, and using Google or another search engine, carry out some research. Use the following prompts to help you:

- **Where in the world is the language spoken?**
- **How old is the language? Does it come from another language(s)? Has the language changed much over time?**
- **How many speakers of the language are there worldwide?**
- **Are there any variations of the language? Do people from different places speak the same language differently?**
- **What *script* is the language written in? How does it appear on the page? For example, English is written in Roman script and Japanese is written in kana.**
- **Find some idioms from your chosen language. Make sure you can explain them.**
- **Is there a specific culture associated with the language? Find out more about the culture.**
- **What are the most famous works of literature which have been written in your chosen language? Who are the writers of these works?**
- **Is the language taught widely in schools where you live? Should it be?**
- **Why might it be an advantage for you to learn this language?**

Using the information you have gathered, prepare a poster and a 3–5-minute presentation for your class.

◆ Assessment opportunities

◆ In this activity you have practised skills that are assessed using Criterion C: Speaking

ACTIVITY: The meaning of language

In pairs, **discuss** the following quotes about language.
- **Interpret** what each quote means.
- **Analyse** the thoughts, feelings, ideas or attitudes about language that are being expressed.
- Which quote do you like the most? **Explain** why.

To have another language is to possess a second soul. *Charlemagne*

If you talk to a man in a language he understands, that goes to his head. If you talk to him in his language, that goes to his heart. *Nelson Mandela*

The limits of my language are the limits of my world. *Ludwig Wittgenstein*

The greatest obstacle to international understanding is the barrier of language. *Christopher Dawson*

You can never understand one language until you understand at least two. *Geoffrey Willans*

One language sets you in a corridor for life. Two languages open every door along the way. *Frank Smith*

What is your 'mother tongue'?

■ What's your mother tongue?

▼ Links to: Sciences

Why do we use the word 'tongue' to talk about language?

It is most likely because the tongue, which is made up of lots of muscles, plays a crucial role in helping us to create the sounds needed to form words.

But how does this marvellous organ know what to do?

About half of your brain is involved in the process. Two areas of the brain are especially important – the Broca area, which controls speaking, and the Wernicke area which helps you to understand words. These two parts are linked by a complicated network that starts to work as soon as you try to speak a word you have read or heard.

First, a message is transmitted to the part of your brain concerned with seeing (if you have read a word) or hearing (if you have heard a word). Then the message is sent to the Broca and Wernicke areas, before an instruction is sent to the areas of the brain which control the movement of your tongue and lips.

And there you have it, a word!

Want to know more? You can find out more about the science behind language by visiting the London Science Museum's website at: **www.sciencemuseum.org.uk/whoami/findoutmore/yourbrain/whatisspecialabouthumanlanguage**

The first language you learn as a child is known as your *mother tongue*. We use the word 'tongue' not only to describe the organ which helps us to form words, but as a synonym for the word 'language'. Your mother tongue, therefore, is the language that you acquire from listening to and communicating with your parents and siblings. Children who grow up in a bilingual household can have two mother tongues, but unless both languages are spoken in equal measure, one language is likely to dominate.

Is it possible to forget your mother tongue? While it is rare to completely lose your first language, if you go years without speaking it, you might find that you are not as fluent as you once were. This varies from person to person and can also depend on how immersed you become in the new language you have adopted.

But we lose more than just our ability to communicate fluently when we become detached from our mother tongue. Our first language is our way of accessing the culture and heritage of our place of origin. By speaking in our mother tongue, we not only keep the language alive but through this we remain connected to our families and communities, and can better understand our histories. The languages we speak are part of our individual and collective identities, and for this reason it is important that we do not lose our mother tongue.

ACTIVITY: Can you lose your tongue?

The languages we speak are bound to our identities. For some, their mother tongue is more than just a language that they speak – it connects them to their homes, their cultures and their families.

In pairs or groups of three, **discuss** the following:

- **What is your mother tongue?**
- **Is it possible to forget your mother tongue? If so, how might this happen?**
- **Can you have more than one mother tongue? Explain why or why not.**
- **Why is your mother tongue important?**
- **Look at the comic strip below and identify the message the artist is trying to convey.**

Now visit this website to read what others have to say about their mother tongues, and then answer the questions which follow: www.bbc.co.uk/news/magazine-28022790

1 Which mother tongue languages feature in the text?
2 **Identify** the factors mentioned in the text which can lead to people becoming less fluent in their mother tongues.
3 How do the people in the text feel about their loss of fluency? Are the reactions mixed? Do they all feel the same?
4 What problems do some of the people in the text face when they are required to communicate in their mother tongue?
5 Can you relate to any of their experiences? **Discuss** with a partner or group.

ITCHY FEET

Welcome home! How's life abroad been treating you?

Great! It's been a good, uh, life ... uh, you know. A good life thing.

Experience?

Yes! Exactly. It's great to see things from a new, um, standing ... place?

Perspective?

Right! Perspective. But it's always nice to come home and eat homemade, uh, you know. Life ... stuff.

Food. Exactly how much English have you forgotten?

I think I need a refresher class.

© 2014 – Malachi Rempen

www.itchyfeetcomic.com

ACTIVITY: Learning experiences

Think about what you have learnt from reading about other people's experiences as bilingual speakers.

Use the online article in the previous activity to reflect on your own experience of learning a new language.

Think back to the start of your language-learning journey. On your own, write down some adjectives to **describe** your feelings when you first started learning a new language.

Share your adjectives with a partner or group. Did you have any words in common?

In pairs, **discuss** some of the challenges you have faced while learning a new language. **Discuss** how you overcame these challenges.

Would you recommend learning a new language to someone else your age? Why? What do you think the advantages are?

How can you make sure that you do not lose your mother tongue?

Now, on your own, write a short account of your experiences as a language learner. Make sure you **organize** your writing using paragraphs.

When should I use capital letters?

You will have noticed in this chapter that languages, such as English and Urdu, start with a capital letter. This is because they are **proper nouns**.

To make your writing accurate, you should know when to use capital letters and when not to.

The following should all begin with a capital letter. For each one, come up with your own examples:

- Names of **people** (and their titles), for example: Charles Dickens, Barack Obama, Prince Charles
- Names of **places**, for example: Africa, London, the Netherlands
- **Languages**, for example: Latin, English, Japanese
- Names of **companies**, for example: Disney, Samsung, Pepsi
- **Nationalities**, for example: British, Indonesian, Australian
- Major words in the **titles** of books and films, for example: *Harry Potter and the Philosopher's Stone*, *Star Wars*
- **Days of the week** and **months of the year**, for example: Monday, July
- **Historical periods** and **events**, for example: the First World War, the Great Fire of London
- **Beginning of a new sentence**, for example: There are over 6000 languages spoken worldwide. We should learn as many of them as possible!
- The **pronoun *I***, for example: I like learning new languages.

ACTIVITY: Capital letters

■ ATL

- Reflection skills: Develop new skills, techniques and strategies for effective learning

Correct the short passage below by adding or removing capital letters.

```
juan and lucinda like Travelling to new
places. last july they visited japan where
they spent three Weeks. while they were
there, they tried lots of new dishes
and visited many beautiful temples. they
tried to practise their japanese every
opportunity they got. one of the places
they visited was hiroshima, the first
place in the world to be the target of a
Nuclear bomb. the Bomb was dropped by the
americans during the second world war.
```

◆ Assessment opportunities

- In this activity you have practised skills that are assessed using Criterion D: Writing

So far in this chapter we have learnt what a language is and why language is so important. We have considered ways in which we can communicate ideas without words, and have conducted some research about a language of our choice. In addition, we have explored some of the challenges that bilingual speakers can face and have reflected on our own experiences as language learners.

What advantages are there to being able to speak more than one language?

SHOULD WE LEARN TO SPEAK NEW LANGUAGES?

It is true that learning a new language can be a daunting experience. It can be strange to hear new sounds rolling off your tongue for the first time, but the many benefits of being able to speak another language are definitely worth the trouble. The challenge of acquiring new words and perfecting your pronunciation can be incredibly exciting.

Having an additional language can open doors. It may seem a long way away right now, but being able to speak another language can boost your future career prospects and perhaps even make you richer. Research shows that people who use languages in their jobs can earn around 8 per cent more than those who do not. You'd better get studying ...

But that is not all. Scientists now believe that being able to speak another language can be good for your health by boosting your brainpower and slowing down the rate at which your brain ages. In fact, studies show that having a grasp of a different language actually improves your ability to use your first language.

We live in an increasingly globalized world and the ability to communicate in another language can be a huge advantage. As travellers, being able to speak to people in their own tongues can enrich our experiences of another culture. As students, we can access literature in the language it was originally written in – a huge advantage as some things are undoubtedly lost in translation. Most importantly, we can use language to reach out to others and build new relationships.

ACTIVITY: What are the British like at learning languages?

■ ATL

- Communication skills: Read critically and for comprehension

The British Council is an organization dedicated to developing and improving cultural relationships between the UK and the rest of the world.

LearnEnglish Teens is a British Council initiative set up to help teenagers from around the world learn English. You can find some great resources on their website: http://learnenglishteens.britishcouncil.org

Read the article on page 61, taken from the LearnEnglish Teens website. Then answer the following questions:

1 What percentage of the British population speak only English? What is your opinion about this?
2 Why don't more British students continue to study a foreign language past the age of 14? **Identify** the two possible reasons given in the article. Is this also the case in your country? Why do you think this is problematic?
3 How do the British government plan to solve this problem? Do you think this is a good idea? Why or why not? How old were you when you began to learn a new language?
4 Since this article was published, many primary schools in the UK have started teaching foreign languages. What might this mean for Britain in the future?

5 Why is Mandarin Chinese one of the new languages that British schools are being encouraged to offer?

6 How do British students feel about learning Mandarin? Is this a language you would be interested in learning? If so, why?

EXTENSION

It is not uncommon for countries to have organizations which promote their language and culture. Carry out some research to find out if your country has an organization dedicated to developing and improving cultural relations with other countries.

◆ Assessment opportunities

◆ In this activity you have practised skills that are assessed using Criterion B: Reading

---

http://learnenglishteens.britishcouncil.org

Languages

How many languages can you speak? British people are generally not very good language learners. In a recent survey, 62% of the population only speak English!

If you're reading this, then you're probably studying English. Maybe you speak a couple of other languages, too. What are the British like when it comes to learning languages?

Statistics

Brits are famous for not speaking foreign languages. According to a survey published by the European Commission, this bad reputation is totally justified. The results of the survey state that the British are officially the worst language learners in Europe! Let's look at some statistics.

62% of people surveyed can't speak any other language apart from English. 38% of Britons speak at least one foreign language, 18% speak two and only 6% of the population speak three or more.

The European Union average showed that 56% speak at least one foreign language, 28% speak at least two and 11% speak three or more.

The survey confirmed that English was the most widely-spoken foreign language: 51% of EU citizens can have a conversation in English.

School

Learning a foreign language is not a popular option at school in Britain. In UK schools it is common for children to not start studying a foreign language until the age of 11 and many students give up languages completely at 14. So why don't young people continue with languages at school? Research suggests that students think that it is more difficult to get good grades in languages than in other subjects such as science or history. The British government is now looking at different ways to improve language learning at school. One idea is to start much younger; there are plans to introduce foreign languages from the age of five.

Which languages?

Another plan is to give school children more choice. The languages traditionally studied in British schools have been French, Spanish and German. Now the government is encouraging teachers to expand the range of languages taught to include Arabic, Mandarin and Urdu.

Mandarin Chinese is predicted to become the second most popular foreign language learned in UK schools. It is already studied by more children than German or Russian. Only French and Spanish are more popular. Gareth from Wales says 'I am learning Chinese and find it fun.' Another student, Thomas from London, says 'Just telling people that I learn Mandarin impresses people. Even having a very basic level gives you an advantage.' Brighton College has become the first independent school to make Mandarin a compulsory foreign language. Its headmaster Richard Cairns said, 'One of my key tasks is to make sure pupils are equipped for the realities of the 21st century. One of those realities is that China has the fastest-growing economy in the world.'

It may be an ambitious task to change the Brits' attitude to learning languages but the government is determined to try!

Taken from **http://learnenglishteens.britishcouncil.org/uk-now/read-uk/languages**

ACTIVITY: Why learn another language?

There are lots of fantastic reasons to learn a new language. In this activity, we will find out what some of them are.

Look carefully at the multimodal text below and then answer the questions about it.

Why have the writers used a question for the heading?

What is the message of the poster?

Identify the target audience. **Justify** your answer, making reference to the visual elements in the poster.

How might this help engage the target audience?

WHY LEARN ANOTHER LANGUAGE?
BECAUSE...

It can raise your grades in other subjects.

You've always wanted to be an international spy, right?

Your future best friend may speak it.

Identify the two verbs in this sentence. Which do you think is more powerful? **Comment** on its effect.

It can help you conquer those bubble tests.

A B C D
A B C D
A B C D

The bigger your world is, the bigger your heart.

It makes you more creative.

How does the text in the poster link to the images?

What is the effect of the repetition used in the text inside the heart?

It's good for your brain.

It can help you get into your dream college.

It can help you land an awesome job.

middlebury
interactive languages
www.middleburyinteractive.com

WE are TEACHERS
www.weareteachers.com

Identify the adjective in this sentence. **Comment** on the effect it might have on the target audience.

Now, in pairs or groups of three, **discuss** which IB learner profile attributes you could develop by learning a new language.

◆ Assessment opportunities

◆ In this activity you have practised skills that are assessed using Criterion B: Reading

Comparative and superlative adjectives

Adjectives which end in 'er' are called **comparative adjectives** or comparatives. Comparative adjectives help us to compare nouns.

They are formed by adding 'er' to the adjective, for example:
- big + er = bigger
- long + er = longer

For some adjectives, this rule doesn't work, so you have to add the word 'more' in front of the adjective. For example:
- fortunate – more fortunate (not fortunater!)
- beautiful – more beautiful (not beautifuler!)

Can you find an example like this in the text on the poster on page 62?

Superlative adjectives help us to grade nouns and say the noun is the most of that quality it could possibly be.

These are formed by adding 'est' to the adjective, for example:
- cold + est = coldest
- small + est = smallest

As with comparatives, for some adjectives this rule doesn't apply. Instead, you have to add the word 'most' before the adjective. For example:
- expensive – most expensive (not expensivest!)

Some adjectives are irregular, for example:
- good – better – best
- bad – worse – worst

Did you know that a person who can speak a number of languages at a high level is known as a *polyglot*?

Timothy Doner is a student at Harvard University who can fluently speak over 20 different languages!

You can find out more about his amazing ability by watching this video: **www.youtube.com/watch?v=Km9-DiFaxpU**

Should English be the universal language?

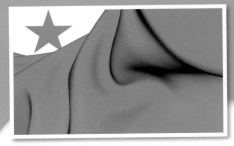

■ The Esperanto flag – the green is said to symbolize hope, the white symbolizes peace and the five-pointed star represents the five continents

Imagine if there was a language that was spoken and understood by people from all over the world, a language which could unite us all – a universal language. In theory, a universal language seems to be the ideal solution to breaking down communication barriers and making the world a smaller place. But in practice, how would it work?

The first obstacle would be deciding on which one of the many thousands of languages spoken in the world today should be the universal language. Should it be the language that currently has the greatest number of speakers worldwide? Or the language which is spoken in most parts of the world already?

Many people perceive English to be the universal language. The spread of the English language owes much to the British Empire and it is now the official language in lots of countries worldwide. It is also relatively easy to learn. But just because it is widespread, should it be the universal language?

There is also a risk that a universal language could displace existing languages. Yes, there are many advantages to having a universal language, but linguistic unity should not come at the expense of other languages. Our language diversity makes the world a more interesting place and it would be a shame for us to lose this.

ACTIVITY: What about a new language?

■ **ATL**

■ Media literacy skills: Interacting with media to use and create ideas and information

What about creating a new language that would make it easy for us to communicate with one another without necessarily sharing a mother tongue? Sounds like a great idea, right? Well, in 1887, a man called Ludwik Lejzer Zamenhof from Poland did just that! He created a new language called Esperanto. Today it is spoken by millions of people worldwide.

Find out more by watching this video and then answer the questions which follow: **www.youtube. com/watch?v=INCr1bV8kGk**

1 **Why did Zamenhof invent Esperanto? What inspired him to do so?**

2 **Infer why the people in the video were able to understand the phrases in Esperanto. What did they notice about the language?**
3 **Evaluate what the advantages of learning Esperanto at school might be.**
4 **How did the parents of the children at the primary school in the video feel about them being taught Esperanto?**
5 **How can Esperanto become a first language?**
6 **What does Terry say are the good things about being able to speak Esperanto?**
7 **What is your opinion about Esperanto? Do you think it is a good idea? Should it be the universal language? Discuss in pairs or groups of three.**

◆ Assessment opportunities

◆ In this activity you have practised skills that are assessed using Criterion A: Listening

ACTIVITY: Borrowed words

Languages are constantly evolving and the English language is no exception. Every year hundreds of new words are added to the Oxford English Dictionary – some new entries in 2016 included *dopiaza*, the name of a curry dish from South India, and *splendiferous*, a wonderful adjective coined by children's writer Roald Dahl. (The year 2016 marked the centenary of Dahl's birth.)

ℹ️ **coined**: from the verb *coin*, which means to invent a new word or phrase.

centenary: the hundredth anniversary of something

You may be surprised to learn that many of the words used in the English language are not really English at all. They have been 'borrowed' from other languages.

Can you think how or why borrowed words might have entered the English language? **Discuss** with a partner or in a group.

In pairs, look at the list of 'English' words below. Can you guess which country or language they originated from?

algebra	diesel	rodeo
ballet	ebony	safari
bungalow	gym	shampoo
canoe	karaoke	
canyon	ketchup	

Still not sure about some of them? Use Google or another search engine to find their origins. You could make a world map and write the words in their country of origin to display in your classroom.

Are there any words in your language which have been borrowed from another language? Or perhaps words from your language which have been borrowed by other languages?

▼ Links to: Individuals and societies: History – The British Empire

Bangle, bazaar, curry, doolally, jungle – these are just a few of the words the English language acquired during the British occupation of India. The British occupied India for nearly 400 years. They ruled between 1757 and 1858 under the British East India Company, and from 1858 to 1947 under the British Crown.

You can learn more about how the British gained control of India by watching this short video: **www.bbc.co.uk/programmes/p0167gdj**

India was just one country or 'colony' which formed the British Empire. An empire is a group of countries which are ruled over by a single monarch or ruling power. The British Empire, at its peak, was the largest empire in history.

Colonisation – the process by which countries seize control of other territories – is one of the reasons why new vocabulary is introduced into a language.

Take action: How can I make a difference?

- We have already seen the value of being plurilingual. Let's now look at ways we can convince others to help us foster a culture of language learning in our schools and communities.

- **Language swap**: Buddy up with someone who has a different mother tongue from you. Ask them to teach you how to have a basic conversation in their language. In exchange, you can help them to learn your language.

- **Language-learning blog**: Ask a teacher to help you set up a blog where you can share your experiences of learning a new language. You could start by posting the piece you wrote earlier in this chapter. Invite others to contribute and exchange helpful tips.

- **Celebrate International Mother Language Day**: Get your school to participate in the celebrations on 21 February to celebrate the linguistic diversity at your school. For more ideas, visit the UN website at: **www.un.org/en/events/motherlanguageday/**

INTERNATIONAL MOTHER LANGUAGE DAY

■ International Mother Language Day is a worldwide event held on 21 February to promote awareness of linguistic and cultural diversity and multilingualism

SOME SUMMATIVE TASKS TO TRY

Use these tasks to apply and extend your learning in this chapter. These tasks are designed so that you can evaluate your learning at different levels of achievement in the Language acquisition criteria.

THIS TASK CAN BE USED TO EVALUATE YOUR LEARNING IN CRITERION B TO PHASE 3

Task 1: International Mother Language Day

- Look at this multimodal text and then answer the following questions.
- Use your own words as much as possible.
- Do not use translating devices or dictionaries for this task.
- You will have 60 minutes to complete this task.

1 What kind of organization has produced this poster and for what purpose? (strands i and ii)
2 **Analyse** how the text in the poster links to the image. (strand ii)
3 **Evaluate** how the designers have tried to make the poster eye-catching and appealing. (strand ii)
4 Who do you think the target audience for this poster is? **Explain** why. (strand ii)
5 **Analyse** the message the poster is trying to convey. (strand iii)
6 **Interpret** how the message been presented in the poster. (strands i and ii)
   a What are the visual features?
   b What are the textual features?
7 Where might you expect to see a poster like this? (strand i)
8 **Identify** the benefits of learning things in your mother tongue. Can you think of any disadvantages? (strand iii)
9 Do you think it is important that we celebrate this event? **Explain** why. Is International Mother Language Day celebrated in your country? How is the occasion celebrated? (strand iii)
10 **Analyse** how your mother tongue helps to shape your individual identity. (strand iii)

INTERNATIONAL MOTHER LANGUAGE DAY 21 FEBRUARY 2012

United Nations
Educational, Scientific and
Cultural Organization

Learning in a language they can understand is vital for children to enjoy their right to quality education. Mother Tongue and Multilingual Education are key to reducing discrimination, promoting inclusion and improving learning outcomes for all.

www.unesco.org/education

Task 2: Dying languages

■ Visit this website and read the article: **www.bbc.co.uk/news/ magazine-11304255**

■ Then answer the following questions, using your own words as much as possible.

■ Refer as closely as possible to the article, **justifying** your answers and giving examples when required.

■ Do not use translating devices or dictionaries for this task.

■ You will have 60 minutes to complete this task.

1 How many languages are estimated to be lost every year? (strand i)
2 Find a synonym in the article for the word *native*. (strand i)
3 What do you think the purpose of the text is? (strand ii)
4 **Summarize** what Ostler describes as the consequences of losing languages. (strand iii)
5 Why have subheadings been used in the text? (strand ii)
6 **Identify** the argument presented in the text which is against saving dying languages. (strand iii)
7 Why do languages die out? **Explain** your answer, providing evidence from the text. (strand i)
8 According to the article, soon everyone will be speaking English. Is this statement true or false? Support your answer with evidence from the text. (strand i)
9 **Evaluate** how physical location might affect the survival of a language. (strand i)
10 **Identify** one other factor mentioned in the article which may help to keep languages alive today. (strand i)
11 Which word in line 18 does Ostler use to make the language seem alive? Can you **explain** what this word means? (strand i)
12 In the article, Howard suggests that 'globalization will mean that many languages disappear'. What does he mean? Why might globalization cause languages to disappear? Make reference to the text to support your answer. (strand iii)
13 Refer again to Howard's opinion about globalization. Do you agree or disagree? **Explain** why or why not. (strand iii)
14 **Identify** the features that make this text multimodal. (strand iii)
15 How do these multimodal features enhance the text? (strand ii)

Reflection

In this chapter we have explored what language is and how it is linked to our individual **identities**. We have seen how language allows us to **communicate** familiar **messages** in new ways on a global scale and how it can help us build **relationships** with others. We have reflected on our own language-learning experiences and have also considered some of the challenges that bilingual learners face. We have evaluated the advantages of plurilingualism, celebrated linguistic diversity and made a pledge to foster a culture of language learning in our schools.

Use this table to reflect on your own learning in this chapter					
Questions we asked	Answers we found	Any further questions now?			
Factual: What is language? How many languages can you speak? What is your 'mother tongue'?					
Conceptual: What advantages are there to being able to speak more than one language?					
Debatable: Should we learn to speak new languages? Should English be the universal language?					
Approaches to learning you used in this chapter	Description – what new skills did you learn?	How well did you master the skills?			
		Novice	Learner	Practitioner	Expert
Collaboration skills					
Communication skills					
Information literacy skills					
Reflection skills					
Media literacy skills					
Transfer skills					
Learner profile attribute(s)	Reflect on the importance of being a good communicator for your learning in this chapter.				
Communicators					

 Is it raining cats and dogs?

In today's world, there is a need for us to **communicate** a new **message**: as members of a **global community**, it is our responsibility to **sustain** our environment by taking a stand against climate change.

CONSIDER THESE QUESTIONS:

Factual: What is weather? What is climate? What is climate change?

Conceptual: How can weather affect our emotional state? What are our feelings and reactions towards daily and seasonal weather?

Debatable: How can we counter the effects of climate change?

Now **share and compare** your thoughts and ideas with your partner, or with the whole class.

■ 'One can't predict the weather more than a few days in advance.' – Stephen Hawking

○ IN THIS CHAPTER, WE WILL ...

■ **Find out** about reactions towards weather, weather conditions and seasons.

■ **Explore** how different people may experience weather differently.

■ **Take action** to learn how our personal choices can have a positive impact on climate change.

■ These Approaches to Learning (ATL) skills will be useful …

- Communication skills
- Organization skills
- Creative-thinking skills
- Critical-thinking skills
- Collaboration skills
- Information literacy skills
- Transfer skills
- Reflection skills

● We will reflect on this learner profile attribute …

- Thinkers – we apply thinking skills that allow us to tackle complex problems in creative ways.

◆ Assessment opportunities in this chapter:

- Criterion A: Listening
- Criterion B: Reading
- Criterion C: Speaking
- Criterion D: Writing

KEY WORDS

climate	meteorologist
extreme	meteorology
forecast	weather
phenomenon/ phenomena	weather forecaster

What do many of us do when we get up in the morning? Go to the window to see what the weather is like! We need to decide what clothes to wear, and if it is a non-school or non-work day, perhaps what to do for the day.

Day-to-day changes in weather dictate the things we can or cannot do and the way we look at the world.

ACTIVITY: Question starts

■ ATL

- Reflection skills: Consider content
- Creative-thinking skills: Make guesses, ask 'what if' questions and generate testable hypotheses

In pairs, **discuss** what you think makes a good question. Now look at the following question starts. They provide a framework, in other words a tool, for asking good questions:

- **Why ...?**
- **How would it be different if ...?**
- **What are the reasons ...?**
- **Suppose that ...?**
- **What if ...?**
- **What if we knew ...?**
- **What is the purpose of ...?**
- **What would change if ...?**

In pairs, brainstorm a list of at least 12 questions about the topic of weather. Use the question starts above to help you think of interesting questions.

In groups of four, review your brainstormed lists and star the questions that seem the most interesting. Then **select** one or two of the starred questions and **discuss** for a few minutes.

Reflect on the new ideas you now have about the topic that you did not have before.

◆ Assessment opportunities

- In this activity you have practised skills that are assessed using Criterion C: Speaking

Severe weather, such as tornadoes, hurricanes and snowstorms, can disrupt many people's lives because of the destruction they cause. The weather can also have a profound effect on our mood and feelings. Each season has its own charm, but for some it can be difficult to cope with the constant change.

In this chapter we will look in more depth at this complex phenomenon and explore our relationship with weather.

How can weather affect our emotional state?

> 'The sun did not shine. It was too wet to play.
> So we sat in the house. All that cold, cold, wet day.'
> – *Dr Seuss,* The Cat in the Hat

WHAT ARE OUR FEELINGS AND REACTIONS TOWARDS DAILY AND SEASONAL WEATHER?

There is a common belief that the British, in particular, love talking about the weather. And why not? Britain is known for its unpredictable weather conditions – snow in April, rain in July, sunshine in October – the weather there seems to do as it pleases. Perhaps that is why it is so easy for British people to talk about the weather.

But it is not only the British who are guilty of indulging in conversation about the weather – we all do it.

Just watch this short video of writer and comedian Evan Elberson talking about the weather: **www.youtube.com/watch?v=CMxbvPZe48s**

We all experience the weather in some form or another, so it seems natural for us to talk about it. It is an easy, safe topic we can all relate to, perfect for those polite chats to make things less awkward at the bus stop.

■ 'Very unpleasant weather, or the old saying verified "Raining Cats, Dogs and Pitchforks"!', by George Cruikshank, 1820

English for the IB MYP 2: *by Concept*

ACTIVITY: Weather idioms

There are so many words and expressions to describe the weather that it can get a little confusing at times. Let's learn and practise some weather expressions.

Task 1

In Chapter 3 (page 51), we looked at Idiom Dingbats. You might want to go back and review what an idiom is. Then, in pairs, match each weather idiom below with its definition.

1	under the weather	a	not know or understand something
2	break the ice		
3	as right as rain		
4	raining cats and dogs	b	behave in a way that is suspicious or not right
5	come rain or shine	c	whatever happens
6	save for a rainy day	d	look very angry
7	snowed under	e	feel ill
8	under a cloud	f	get angry over something that is not important
9	not have the foggiest (idea)	g	make someone feel less nervous
10	storm in a teacup	h	heavy rain
11	face like thunder	i	feel well again after being ill
		j	have so much to do
		k	put money aside for when you need it

Use this website to check your answers:
http://dictionary.cambridge.org/dictionary/english/

Task 2

In pairs, look at the weather idioms in Task 1 and complete each sentence with a suitable expression.

1 Emilia _____ $50 a month _____.
2 Dakini goes jogging after school _____.
3 Álvaro was in bed with the flu all of last week, but he is _____ now.
4 Taavi _____ about football. He much prefers rugby.
5 Pietro got home late after the party. His father had a _____ when he opened the front door.
6 Maya has gone to bed because she is feeling a bit _____.
7 Zaina is totally _____ with school-work right now. The exams are next week.
8 Pablo had an argument with his best friend yesterday, but it was just a _____.
9 We have to cancel the picnic tomorrow. It's going to _____.
10 On our first day at school, the teacher asked us to play games to _____.
11 Mr Dubois left his job at the bank _____.

Use this website to check your answers:
www.vocabulary.cl/english/weather-idioms.htm

Task 3

Create your own *personal dictionary*. Think about how to **organize** vocabulary to help you to learn new words and phrases. You could consider the following systems:

- • **subject specific**
- • **alphabetical**
- • **general/technical**
- • **social/academic**
- • **English only or bilingual**
- • **antonyms and synonyms**

Using the online dictionary and vocabulary website given in Tasks 1 and 2, **select** new weather expressions to include in your personal dictionary.

ACTIVITY: Why do Brits talk about the weather?

■ ATL

■ Communication skills: Read critically and for comprehension

You are going to read an article called 'Why do Brits talk about the weather so much?'. Before you do, **discuss** the title with a partner. Do people in your country talk about the weather?

Task 1

Visit the following website to read the article and then, in pairs, answer the questions below: www.bbc.com/future/story/20151214-why-do-brits-talk-about-the-weather-so-much

1 Look at the first three paragraphs of the article. **Identify** one word that matches each of the following definitions:
   - boring or dull
   - difficult to explain or understand
   - a person who answers questions in a survey or questionnaire
   - talked about
   - something that deserves to be given attention or should be noticed
   - unusual or strange characteristic
2 **Identify** the features that influence the British weather.
3 Which topics do other nationalities prefer to use to 'break the ice'?
4 **Explain**, using your own words, what *small talk* means.
5 **Interpret** why British people prefer to talk about the weather.
6 Based on the writer's comments, what type of weather can you have over a weekend in Britain?
7 Would you recommend this article to someone else? Why? Why not?

Task 2

The article refers to a haiku poem on weather by the Japanese novelist Natsume Soseki. In pairs, remind yourselves of what a haiku poem is. If you get stuck, use Google or another search engine to help you.

Now it's your turn! Write your own weather haiku poems.

Recite your poems to your classmates.

◆ Assessment opportunities

◆ This activity can be assessed using Criterion B: Reading and Criterion D: Writing

---

ⓘ Did you know that some people are prone to feeling depressed when the weather changes? This disorder is called SAD, which stands for Seasonal Affective Disorder.

To find out more visit the following websites:

www.mind.org.uk/information-support/types-of-mental-health-problems/seasonal-affective-disorder-sad/#.WBIolmNaHzI

www.sada.org.uk/index_2.php

ACTIVITY: Weather in literature and art

ATL

- Communication skills: Read critically and for comprehension
- Creative-thinking skills: Create original works and ideas

The weather has always been a source of inspiration for writers and artists. The weather is an ideal vehicle through which we can express our feelings.

Task 1

Look at the poem below by the American poet Henry Wadsworth. Then, in pairs, **discuss** the questions which follow.

The Rainy Day

The day is cold, and dark, and dreary;
It rains, and the wind is never weary;
The vine still clings to the mouldering wall,
But at every gust the dead leaves fall,
And the day is dark and dreary.

My life is cold, and dark, and dreary;
It rains, and the wind is never weary;
My thoughts still cling to the mouldering past,
But the hopes of youth fall thick in the blast,
And the days are dark and dreary.

Be still, sad heart, and cease repining;
Behind the clouds is the sun still shining;
Thy fate is the common fate of all,
Into each life some rain must fall,
Some days must be dark and dreary.

By Henry Wadsworth

1 **Interpret** the message of the poem.
2 What feelings are associated with the wind and the rain in the poem? **Identify** the language which is used to illustrate these emotions.
3 Is there any hope in the poem? **Identify** the type of weather used to represent this.
4 How does the weather affect your mood? Which type of weather has the greatest impact on how you feel? Do you have a favourite season? **Explain** why it is your favourite season. ➤

Task 2

Now look at the paintings below. In pairs or groups of three, **create** a mind map of words you associate with the type of weather depicted in the paintings, and the emotions they evoke. Make sure you include vocabulary (adjectives and **abstract nouns** – see page 77) related to feelings.

■ 'October extinguished itself in a rush of howling winds and driving rain and November arrived, cold as frozen iron, with hard frosts every morning and icy drafts that bit at exposed hands and faces.' – *Harry Potter and the Order of the Phoenix*, J.K. Rowling

Abstract nouns

Happiness, love, success, wealth – what do these word all have in common?

Besides the fact that they are all things we want in life, all of these words are *abstract nouns*. They are nouns that refer to things which do not exist as material objects – usually ideas and concepts.

A good way to decide whether or not a noun is abstract is to see whether it is something you can experience using the five senses. If you cannot see it, hear it, smell it, touch it or taste it, then it is probably abstract.

Use your mind map words and the paintings above to **create** your own poem about the weather.

Recite and display your poems in the classroom.

◆ Assessment opportunities

- ◆ This activity can be assessed using Criterion B: Reading and Criterion D: Writing

ACTIVITY: Perceive – Know about – Care about

■ **ATL**

■ Reflection skills: Develop new skills, techniques and strategies for effective learning

This routine can help you to **explore** different perspectives and viewpoints as you try to imagine things, events, problems or issues differently.
It can lead to a more creative understanding of a topic and using abstract nouns is one of the tools you can use to achieve this.

Use the following core questions to guide you in this routine:

1 **What can the person or thing *perceive*?**
2 **What might the person or thing *know about* or believe?**
3 **What might the person or thing *care about*?**

In pairs or groups of three, choose one of the paintings on pages 76–77 and generate a list of the various perspectives or points of view reflected in that painting. Choose a particular point of view to embody or talk from, saying what the person perceives, knows about and cares about. It could be the perspective of one of the characters in the image or perhaps you could personify the weather and bring that to life.

From your chosen point of view, talk about what you are experiencing. Take turns to ask each other questions that will help your partner stay in character. Try to draw out his or her point of view.

◆ Assessment opportunities

◆ In this activity you have practised skills that are assessed using Criterion C: Speaking

ACTIVITY: Get creative!

■ **ATL**

■ Transfer skills: Apply skills and knowledge in unfamiliar situations
■ Creative-thinking skills: Create original works and ideas; Use existing works and ideas in new ways

Task 1

Create your own abstract noun vocabulary list using the following prompts:
● **Words to show human qualities and characteristics**
● **Words to show emotions and feelings**

Use an online dictionary such as this to help you: **http://dictionary.cambridge.org/**

Task 2

The figure on page 79 shows a **fictional** map of a city.

In pairs, look at the different places shown and give each one an abstract noun name, for example, *The Park of Hope*.

◆ Assessment opportunities

◆ This activity can be assessed using Criterion D: Writing

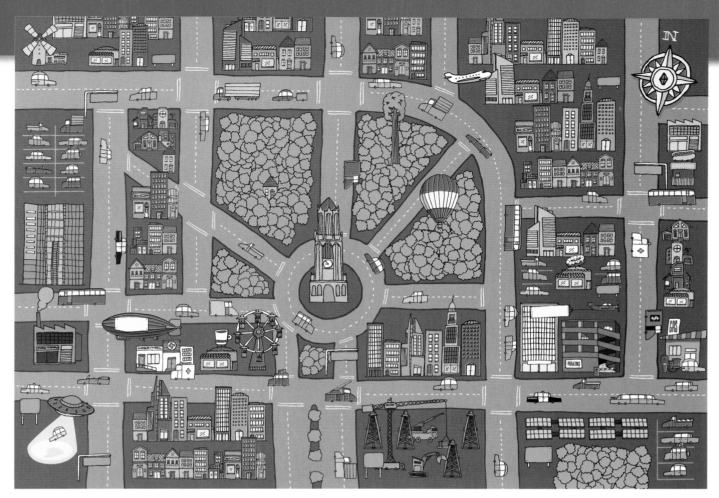

■ What abstract noun names will you give to the places on this map?

EXTENSION: ALWAYS TAKE THE WEATHER WITH YOU

Visit this website and listen carefully to the song *Weather with You* by Crowded House: **www.youtube.com/watch?v=ag8XcMG1EX4**

Listen carefully and, in pairs, **analyse** the reference to Julius Caesar and **explain** what point is being made about the power of the weather.

Weather is a great subject for a song. Do you know any other songs about the weather? **Discuss** with a partner or in a group.

Use Google or another search engine to search for songs about the weather to find some more.

So far in this chapter we have developed a simple understanding of the very complex phenomenon of weather. We have explored how the topic of weather is one which almost everyone can relate to, but have also seen that the way in which we communicate about weather can vary from culture to culture. We have considered the impact that the weather can have on the way that we feel, and have looked at examples of literature and art inspired by the elements.

What is weather?

WHAT IS CLIMATE?

'There is no question that climate change is happening; the only arguable point is what part humans are playing in it.' – David Attenborough

What is *weather*? It is the state of the atmosphere at any given time, including factors such as temperature, precipitation or rain, air pressure and cloud cover. Daily changes in the weather are usually due to winds or storms, while seasonal changes are due to the Earth revolving around the Sun. Climate, however, is not the same as weather. We use *climate* to describe the average pattern of weather over an extended time period for a particular region.

'Rainiest Month in a Decade' and 'Record High Temperatures' are common headlines in newspapers around the world. There are several places that claim to be the 'rainiest spot on Earth' or the 'driest location'. Can you find out where these places might be?

■ Severe storms are interesting features in satellite imagery

Extreme weather is often destructive. Storms such as hurricanes and tornadoes can cause death, devastation and millions of dollars' worth of damage. Prolonged heatwaves and cold spells result in increased illness and death, particularly among the sick, the very young and the elderly. Also, during spells of severe weather, particularly when it is very cold, homeless people or people displaced due to war are particularly vulnerable.

If you are interested in weather, you can study *meteorology*. Weather scientists, called *meteorologists*, use radar and other instruments to locate, track and determine the extent of storms and other types of extreme weather. They issue *forecasts*, as well as warnings of approaching storms, so that people can prepare themselves for bad weather, and sometimes vacate areas that are on high alert and protect buildings. However, sometimes there simply is not enough time to warn communities.

ⓘ Did you know that in the UK, extreme storms are given names? In February 2017 'Storm Doris' swept through the UK causing chaos. Do you think *Doris* is a good name for a storm? Why? Why not?

Visit this website and find out why storms are given names:
www.bbc.co.uk/newsround/ 34581210

If you could name a storm, what name would you choose? Why? Are storms given names in your country?

ACTIVITY: Making sense of weather information

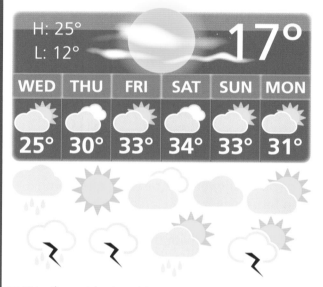

H: 25°
L: 12°

17°

WED	THU	FRI	SAT	SUN	MON
25°	30°	33°	34°	33°	31°

■ Weather widget and icons

A weather widget is a tool that gives information about the current and upcoming weather, in other words, the weather forecast. It is one of the tools that forecasters use to describe the weather for the next day or the week ahead.

In pairs, carry out some research using Google or another search engine to find weather widgets for your local area.

Where can you find weather widgets?

In pairs, look at the different weather icons above and guess the type of weather for each one. Make a list of the different weather elements and then try to **design** your own icons.

Share your icons with your classmates and vote for the best ones.

ACTIVITY: Fact or opinion?

When we speak or write, we can state facts or opinions. So, what is the difference? A *fact* is something that is true and you can prove to other people. An *opinion* is something that you think or believe in, but you cannot prove.

Watch the following video and listen to Bill McKibben talk about climate change: www.youtube.com/watch?v=5KtGg-Lvxso

Now answer the following questions:

1 **Identify** two opinions that the speaker supports with a reason.
2 **Identify** three facts that the speaker supports with evidence.
3 **What do you think about this subject? Write one sentence expressing your opinion and another sentence to explain the reasons for it.**
4 **Share your answers with a partner.**

ACTIVITY: Your research project

What is your project?

Have you ever wondered what clouds are made of? Or how tornadoes are formed and what causes them? The fact is that stepping into the wild world of weather is fascinating! Weather and atmospheric science offer lots of opportunities for interesting projects. There is a wide range of online resources available so you can make your project as easy or as advanced as you like.

You are going to find out about clouds, rain, wind, snow and all kinds of interesting weather phenomena through project work. As part of your research, you will find out the similarities and differences between the weather and climate in your country and another country of your choice. Then why not take it a step further and look at how weather and/or climate impacts on the local flora and fauna?

Look at the articles, images and other materials on the websites below to give you ideas, but remember that it takes more than one article to make a research project.

www.sciencekids.co.nz/weather.html

www3.epa.gov/climatechange/kids/

www.climatecentral.org/videos/category/show/flora_fauna

www.worldclimate.com/

http://whyfiles.org/category/weather-guys/June/?orderby=rand

Choose your research question

Work in groups of three or five to brainstorm ideas and questions about weather and climate. Then **select** an area to focus your project on and **formulate** your research question by selecting a weather phenomenon from the box below.

climate	rain	thunder
clouds	snow	tornadoes
hurricanes	storms	water cycle
lightning	temperature	wind

Narrow your field of research

To help you to answer your research question:

- **Keep focused on the one area you have chosen to research.**
- **Do not try to work with too many different sources – select two or three sources.**
- **Keep a vocabulary list as you work and encounter new words.**

Your research, and the research carried out by your class, will help give you a better understanding of the weather and how unpredictable it can be. You will also learn more about the power of weather and how it can affect the way we live.

Organize and present your project

In your group, plan how you will conduct your research.

As you research, **evaluate** and **select** the key information you want to use. **Create** and share a folder to collate this information through Google drive, Dropbox or another cloud storage that is right for you.

Hints

As you research, make notes on the relevant information that answers your question.

Keep a record of the sources you have used.

Present your research to the class, supported by a PowerPoint, Prezi or poster. Include audio and/or visual material to support your work. Your presentation should be 3–4 minutes long.

At the end of the presentation, allow your classmates to ask questions about your research topic. Give and receive feedback from your peers.

Final task

Submit your research project. You can create a YouTube video or submit your research project as an interactive bio cube.

- **Include evidence of your brainstorming and planning stages.**
- **Conclude by stating your own opinions and experiences if relevant.**
- **Consider making proposals for individual or school community action.**
- **Reference your sources of information, using a recognized system.**

▼ Links to: Sciences; Individuals and societies: Geography

You may have already looked at some of the science behind how weather works in your science and geography lessons. Why not **synthesize** some of your knowledge and carry out a research project.

Think about climate change for your next Science Fair Project. Visit the following website for ideas on how to plan your project: **http://climatekids.nasa.gov/science-fair/**

◆ Assessment opportunities

◆ In this activity you have practised skills that are assessed using Criterion B: Reading and Criteron C: Speaking

ACTIVITY: Why should we care about climate change?

Global warming is one of the major factors responsible for causing climate change. Let's now look at some of the serious consequences of this phenomenon.

In pairs, look at the multimodal text on the next page and then answer the questions below.

1 **Identify** the message the poster is trying to convey.
2 **Identify** the purpose of the poster.
3 **Evaluate** how successfully the designers of the poster convey the message. Consider their use of language in the text and the central image.
4 **Infer** who the target audience is.
5 **Analyse** how the designers create sympathy for people who are suffering from the consequences of climate change. Why do you think this setting was chosen?
6 **Discuss** how the poster makes you feel. **Evaluate** the effect it has on your attitude towards climate change.
7 Are people in your country concerned about climate change? What is being done to combat climate change there?
8 How could you help to raise awareness about climate change and its effects?

CLIMATE CHANGE HURTS

Besides environmental and economic damage,
the ultimate impact of climate change represents a toll
on our most precious resource - human lives and health.

Protecting health from climate change

World Health Organization

www.who.int/phe   www.who.int/globalchange

◼ Climate change has a tremendous impact on human lives

ACTIVITY: A Song of Our Warming Planet

■ ATL

- Information literacy skills: Process data and report results

Scientist often share the latest climate change discoveries through data graphics and images.

Daniel Crawford, a student from the University of Minnesota, USA, came up with an interesting and different idea for interpreting information to raise awareness about climate change.

Watch the following video and then answer the questions below: www.youtube.com/watch?v=5t08CLczdK4

1 In two sentences, **summarize** the purpose and theme of the video.
2 Daniel purposefully uses music in the video. **Evaluate** why you think he does this.
3 What is the purpose of the graph?
4 **Interpret** the information reflected in the graph.
5 **Analyse** what Daniel wants us to feel about climate change. How does he make us understand?
6 **Identify** the setting of the video.
7 **Identify** the intended audience for the video. Why do you think this?
8 What examples does Daniel give to support his viewpoint?
9 Complete this sentence from the video:
   The additional _____ would _____ a series of _____ beyond the _____ of _____ hearing.
10 Can you relate to the footage in the video? Are the opinions familiar to you? If you were to create a video with the same message for young people, what footage would you use?

EXTENSION

In pairs, look at the tables below and then answer the questions which follow.

- **Identify** the purpose of the tables.
- **Analyse** the layout of the tables.
- How do the tables differ from the graph in the video in the first task?
- Write a paragraph to **describe** the weather patterns in the tables.

◆ Assessment opportunities

- ◆ This activity can be assessed using Criterion A: Listening and Criterion D: Writing

! Take action: How can I make a difference?

! The American actor Leonardo DiCaprio is very concerned about climate change. He has been involved in many projects that explore climate change and is active in trying to raise awareness of what must be done to prevent further damage to our planet.

! DiCaprio spent three years making a documentary film, *Before the Flood*, to raise awareness of the damage being done to our planet and the effects of climate change. The film is available to watch for free online at: **http://channel.nationalgeographic.com/before-the-flood/videos/watch-before-the-flood-for-free-everywhere/**

! Arrange a school viewing of *Before the Flood*. After the film, organize a roundtable debate. Use it as a platform to explore ways in which your school can get involved to raise awareness of climate change. Encourage people to think about the daily choices they make and how they can help to make a difference.

! Think about how you might encourage people to become more active. You could:

◆ Make some posters to display around your school. Raise awareness and show others how they can help to make a difference.

◆ Set up a school Environment Club. You could meet regularly to discuss climate change and come up with strategies for your school to become a more environmentally friendly place.

◆ Visit the following website for ideas about how to be part of the solution: **www3.epa.gov/climatechange/kids/solutions/index.html**

■ A woman assesses the destruction of her home caused by a tsunami

SOME SUMMATIVE TASKS TO TRY

Use these tasks to apply and extend your learning in this chapter. These tasks are designed so that you can evaluate your learning at different levels of achievement in the Language acquisition criteria.

THIS TASK CAN BE USED TO EVALUATE YOUR LEARNING IN CRITERION D TO CAPABLE LEVEL

Task 1

Look at the images above and opposite and then respond to *one* of the following prompts:
■ Imagine you are one of the people in one of the images. Write a passage to **describe** what is happening, how you feel about it and why.
■ You should aim to write 200–250 words.

You will have 45 minutes to complete this task.

■ A homeless man is forced to brave the harsh winter weather as he prepares to spend another night out in the cold

■ Floods can have devastating consequences and can have effects on the economy, environment and people

Task 2: Interactive oral – climate change

- You will engage in a discussion with your teacher about climate change issues by presenting a global warming problem and responding to questions about possible solutions, using the prompts below.
- The discussion should include a personal response to the issue and ways in which you can take action to ameliorate the problem.
- You are expected to speak for 3–4 minutes.

Look again at the images on pages 88 and 89.
1 What do you think is one of the most important climate change issues facing our planet?
2 How can people be encouraged to take action to reduce the effects of this problem on the environment?
3 Why do you think this issue is important?
4 What is a possible solution? Why do you think this solution would work?
5 What can you do to help solve the problem?

Reflection

In this chapter we have explored the topic of weather and our various **purposes** for **communicating** about it. We have considered in depth our complex relationship with the elements and the tremendous impact they can have on our material existence and internal emotions. We have looked at the devastating effects of climate change and our role as **global** citizens to combat this so we can **sustain** our environment for future generations. We have tried to convey this crucial **message** through our writing.

Use this table to reflect on your own learning in this chapter					
Questions we asked	Answers we found	Any further questions now?			
Factual: What is weather? What is climate? What is climate change?					
Conceptual: How can weather affect our emotional state? What are our feelings and reactions towards daily and seasonal weather?					
Debatable: How can we counter the effects of climate change?					
Approaches to learning you used in this chapter	Description – what new skills did you learn?	How well did you master the skills?			
		Novice	Learner	Practitioner	Expert
Communication skills					
Organization skills					
Creative-thinking skills					
Critical-thinking skills					
Collaboration skills					
Information literacy skills					
Transfer skills					
Reflection skills					
Learner profile attribute(s)	Reflect on the importance of being a good thinker for your learning in this chapter.				
Thinkers					

5 What if everybody looked the same?

For centuries, we have used **external cultural signs** as a vehicle for **personal and cultural expression**. In today's world, however, teenagers are being constantly bombarded with **messages** about how they should look and dress, and are under immense pressure to conform to certain **points of view** about beauty.

CONSIDER THESE QUESTIONS:

Factual: What is fashion?

Conceptual: Does it matter what we look like? How can we express ourselves through the way we look? How does the way we dress reflect who we are? How have our notions of beauty changed over time?

Debatable: What is beauty? To what extent is our idea of true beauty influenced by our environment? Can the pursuit of ideal beauty be dangerous? What price are we willing to pay for ideal beauty?

Now **share and compare** your thoughts and ideas with your partner, or with the whole class.

■ How do people use their appearance to express their identities?

IN THIS CHAPTER, WE WILL …

- **Find out** what beauty is and how our perceptions of beauty vary from culture to culture.
- **Explore** the ways in which we use fashion and beauty as a means of personal expression.
- **Take action** to raise awareness of some of the dangerous consequences of the pursuit of beauty.

We will reflect on this learner profile attribute …

- Balanced – we understand the importance of balancing different aspects of our lives – intellectual, physical and emotional – to achieve well-being for ourselves and others.

These Approaches to Learning (ATL) skills will be useful …

- Communication skills
- Collaboration skills
- Affective skills
- Information literacy skills

Assessment opportunities in this chapter:

- Criterion A: Listening
- Criterion B: Reading
- Criterion C: Speaking
- Criterion D: Writing

KEY WORDS

accessories	diversity
adornment	fashion
apparel	garment
beauty	

ACTIVITY: The Ugly Duckling

ATL

- Communication skills: Make inferences and draw conclusions

Visit the following website and read the story 'The Ugly Duckling' by Hans Christian Andersen: www.andersen.sdu.dk/vaerk/hersholt/TheUglyDuckling_e.html

While you read, consider the:
- **intended target audience**
- **message of the story**
- **presentation of the 'ugly' duckling.**

Now, in pairs, share your thoughts about the story and **discuss**:
- **What does the story reveal about our attitudes towards beauty?**
- **Is it important for children to read this story? Justify your response.**
- **Think about some other fairy tales that you read as a child. How is the theme of beauty explored in these stories? What effect might they have on the intended target audience?**

Assessment opportunities

- In this activity you have practised skills that are assessed using Criterion B: Reading

What is beauty?

DOES IT MATTER WHAT WE LOOK LIKE?

■ How would you define beauty?

True beauty is difficult to define. For centuries, philosophers and thinkers have tried to do so, but it is almost impossible because we are all different and we all have different points of view. Human beauty, in particular, is the subject of much debate and discussion in today's world, perhaps more so than ever before. It is this type of beauty, and the lengths that we go to in order to attain it, that we will explore in this chapter.

They say that beauty lies in the eye of the beholder – that our perception of what is and is not beautiful is personal and subjective. Yet many of us aspire to look a certain way because of what we have been led to believe is beautiful within our societies. Our ideas about beauty have evolved over time and continue to do so. They also vary from culture to culture

and change as we grow older. One thing is certain, however – with people spending billions on beauty products and clothes each year – our obsession with the way we look is here to stay.

But why should we care about how we look? Does our physical appearance have a significant impact on our lives or our success in the wider world? Do our choices about how we adorn our bodies with clothes and accessories reveal and express something deeper about our personalities and identities? Or does what is inside us matter more than the face we show to the world?

In this chapter we will explore our preoccupation with beauty and fashion, and find out whether beauty is only skin deep.

ACTIVITY: Defining beauty

ATL

■ Collaboration skills: Build consensus

We all have different views on what beauty is, but let's see if we can come up with a definition of our own. In pairs or groups of three, agree on a definition for the word *beauty* and write it down.

Now watch the following video and **discuss** the questions below: www.youtube.com/watch?v=jKTZAsDVkzs

- Do you think that girls are under more pressure than boys to be 'beautiful'?
- Do you agree with the women in the video that girls are exposed to this pressure from an early age? How does this make you feel?

- **Summarize** the message of the video. **Evaluate** whether the message is a positive or negative one.
- Choose your favourite quote from the video and **explain** why you have chosen it.
- What is your opinion – does beauty matter? How often do you think about the way you look?
- **Compare** your definition of beauty to the way in which it is defined by the women in the video.

◆ Assessment opportunities

◆ In this activity you have practised skills that are assessed using Criterion A: Listening

■ Where does the pressure to look beautiful come from?

How can we express ourselves through the way we look?

HOW DOES THE WAY WE DRESS REFLECT WHO WE ARE?

In William Shakespeare's *Hamlet*, the character Polonius advises his son, Laertes, to take care when choosing his clothes:

'For the apparel oft proclaims the man,'

In other words, Polonius believes that 'clothes make the man'. Wise words … or are they? How important are our clothes and what do they reveal about us? Does it really matter what we wear?

We are all different, inside and out, and this is what makes us unique. It follows, therefore, that the way we present ourselves to the world should reflect this and this is where clothes, make-up and accessories come into play.

The way in which we choose to adorn our bodies can say a lot about us. Our clothes can be used to signify our wealth and status. The accessories we wear can be symbols of our faith or connect us with a certain group or community to which we belong. We can make certain choices about what we wear as an act of rebellion or simply to reflect our taste in music or other interests. Sometimes what we consider beautiful or attractive is influenced by the culture of the places we are from or where we live. For some, donning certain types of clothing or wearing make-up can help us to feel more confident about ourselves, while for others, comfort is the most important factor.

Whatever the reason behind our choices, what we wear conveys a message about ourselves. Clothing can be a wonderful means for personal expression!

Style is a way to say who you are without having to speak. *Rachel Zoe*

In order to be irreplaceable one must always be different. *Coco Chanel*

Vain trifles as they seem, clothes have, they say, more important offices than to merely keep us warm. They change our view of the world and the world's view of us. *Virginia Woolf*

Fashion should be a form of escapism, and not a form of imprisonment. *Alexander McQueen*

Don't be into trends. Don't make fashion own you, but you decide what you are, what you want to express by the way you dress and the way you live. *Gianni Versace*

Fashion is instant language. *Miuccia Prada*

ACTIVITY: Speaking about style

■ ATL

■ Collaboration skills: Listen actively to other perspectives and ideas

In pairs, **discuss** the quotes on these two pages about fashion and style.

- **Interpret** what each quote means.
- **Analyse** the thoughts, feelings, ideas or attitudes about style that are being expressed in each quote.
- Which quote do you like the most? **Explain** why.

◆ Assessment opportunities

◆ In this activity you have practised skills that are assessed using Criterion B: Reading and Criterion C: Speaking

ACTIVITY: What do your clothes say about you?

■ ATL

- Affective skills: Emotional management: Practise strategies to reduce stress and anxiety; Practise strategies to prevent and eliminate bullying

Before you begin, **discuss** the following in pairs:
- **Have you ever felt that someone judged you based on your clothing or appearance? How did this make you feel?**
- **Have you ever made a judgement about someone else based on their clothing or general appearance? Why did you do this?**

Now read the statements on this page and opposite and, in pairs or groups of three, **discuss** and complete the following tasks:

1 **Identify** the reasons behind some of the beauty and clothing choices that these people make. See if you can **recognize** any similarities or differences between the statements.
2 Who can you relate to the most? **Explain** why.
3 Are you influenced by any of the reasons in the statements? Why do you dress the way you do? Does your clothing reveal something about your personal or cultural identity?
4 Write your own paragraph, like those on this page and opposite, to **explain** your personal style.

◆ Assessment opportunities

- ◆ In this activity you have practised skills that are assessed using Criterion B: Reading and Criterion D: Writing

I don't want to look like everyone else. That's boring. For me, fashion is all about pushing boundaries and experimenting. People think fashion is just for women, but men can express themselves through clothes as well. I started to wear skirts because I think they look cool and can sometimes be more comfortable. In a way it's a return to the ways of old Japan when men used to wear *yukatas*, a garment which looks a bit like a dress. In the more fashionable cities it's quite common to see men wearing skirts these days, so I have to work harder to make myself stand out. *Shuya, 19, student*

I'd describe my personal style as 'quirky' or 'vintage'. My favourite era for fashion is the 1940s and if I had a time machine I'd be there in an instant! Of course, I know it was a turbulent time for much of the world because of the war, but I'm so impressed by the way the men and women still managed to look so pristine and well put together. I'm a school teacher, but music is my true love and I'm in a jazz band so my style really suits my image as a singer. People often comment on my appearance and ask me where I get my stuff from. Well, I buy most of my clothes from vintage clothes shops or online. But sometimes, if you look hard enough, you can find some real gems in charity shops. *Iamara, 34, teacher and jazz singer*

I hate the idea of just blending in. My friends say I have a 'big' personality so my clothes have to reflect this! My mother is from Kenya and even though I was born here in Denmark, I feel a strong connection to the African culture. One of the ways in which I can express this is through my clothes. I like bold prints and bright colours, but the style and fit of my clothing has to be understated and classic (which is quite typical of Scandinavian style), so I guess I'm using clothes and accessories to fuse together the two worlds I belong to. *Mia, 20, student*

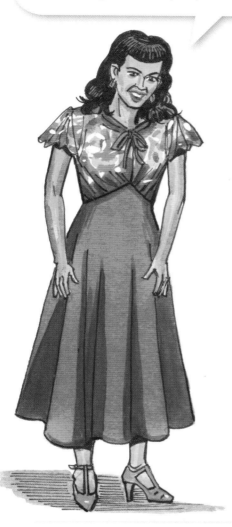

People make assumptions about me all the time. If they just took the time to talk to me or ask me questions about why I choose to wear a headscarf, they'd realize that I'm an average teenage girl. I live and breathe fashion which is why I started my blog last year. Some people think that wearing a scarf takes away a person's individuality. I totally disagree. Yes, it reflects my religious and cultural identity, but at the end of the day it's just an accessory like any other, and you can be as creative with it as you like. I own about 125 different scarves in every print and colour under the sun … it's becoming quite an addiction actually! *Hanya, 15, student and fashion blogger*

So far in this chapter we have learnt about what beauty is and how difficult it can be to define. We have explored how fashion and beauty can be used by people as a way of personal expression. In addition to this, we have considered our own ideas about beauty and have evaluated the messages our clothes communicate about us.

To what extent is our idea of true beauty influenced by our environment?

HOW HAVE OUR NOTIONS OF BEAUTY CHANGED OVER TIME?

■ Beauty around the globe: (clockwise from top right) Kim Kardashian, 'Giraffe' women of Myanmar, Wodaabe men ready for the annual Gerewol festival where they decorate themselves to impress the women, a Geisha in Japan, Masai women from Kenya

Our environment has a profound influence on the choices we make about what we wear. Where we live and the attitudes of the people we are surrounded by can help shape our ideas about what is beautiful and what is not.

Our exposure to different cultures can also have an impact on our notions of beauty by challenging our existing points of view. In our increasingly globalized world, we see evidence of this daily in the clothes people wear and the way in which they adorn their bodies. Take henna painting, for example – a body art that originated in the Middle East and South Asia – which has found its way into the western world as an alternative to tattoos.

Fashion and beauty trends from the past can also teach us a great deal about people from bygone eras. Through their clothes and make-up, we can learn about their attitudes, beliefs and values. History shows us that fashion is resilient – even in times of instability, people have used clothing to express themselves, perhaps even to escape the horrors taking place in the world around them.

Fashion is always evolving and so are our ideas about beauty. In the past, trends were more uniform, but in our world today anything goes! In this section, we will explore and celebrate the history and diversity of fashion and beauty.

■ Moroccan henna tattoo

ACTIVITY: 100 years of ...

Find out how beauty and fashion trends have evolved over the ages in your home country.

WatchCut Videos have created a series of videos which document the changing fashion and beauty trends in over 20 different countries around the world. Spanning a number of decades, the videos cover trends for both men and women, and are lively and fun to watch. More importantly, the videos give us an incredibly valuable insight into the culture of these places and how this can influence the way we look.

Go to the following website to see the selection of '100 years of ...' WatchCut Videos: **www.youtube.com/playlist?list=PLJic7bfGlo3qlgmccaaNAXTChp_Ny8CE4**

In pairs, watch some of the videos and then complete the following tasks.

1 Choose one of the countries explored in the videos – it might be your home country, a place that you have an interest in, or one where you felt the most radical changes in beauty took place.
2 **Discuss** your thoughts and feelings about what you saw in the video. What did you find interesting? What surprised you the most?
3 Use the internet to carry out some research about the historical event(s) which were taking place during each of the decades shown in the video. **Synthesize** the information you gather in two or three sentences.
4 **Evaluate** the impact these events might have had on fashion/beauty trends in the country at the time. For example, in the video on Iran, what happened to fashion and beauty in the 1980s? What historical events might have triggered this? Find out.
5 **Present** your findings to the whole class.

Has anyone ever told you not to judge a book by its cover? Well, the same goes for people!

Although our first impressions of people are often based on their body language, facial expressions or what they might be wearing, we should reserve our judgement about them until we have had the chance to get to know them. Sadly, in the past not everyone thought this way, and judging people by their physical appearance was treated like a science.

Physiognomy – the study of a person's facial features – gained popularity in the eighteenth and nineteenth centuries. People believed that a person's face could reveal things about their personality, intelligence and even how likely they were to commit a crime!

Thankfully, in today's world, we know better than to judge a person based on the way they look.

Have you ever heard anyone describe a book or film as *highbrow*? Well, the root of this expression lies in *phrenology* – another dubious 'science' from the past – which involved drawing inferences about the character and intelligence of a person based on the shape and size of their head.

Use Google or another search engine to find out what the expressions **highbrow**, **lowbrow** and **middlebrow** mean.

In pairs, using what you have discovered in your searches, **infer** what people during the eighteenth and nineteenth centuries might have believed about the size of a person's brow.

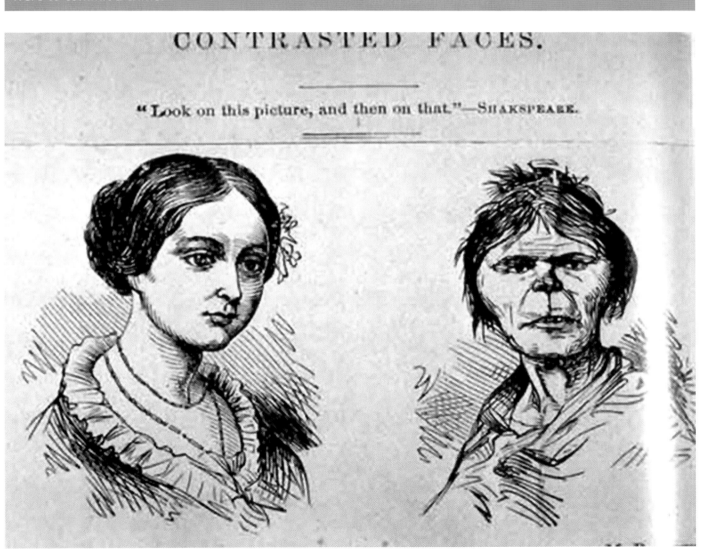

■ People once believed that you could judge a person's character based on their physical appearance

Can the pursuit of ideal beauty be dangerous?

WHAT PRICE ARE WE WILLING TO PAY FOR IDEAL BEAUTY?

In a world where we are bombarded by images of perfection on a day-to-day basis, it is easy for young people to lose sight of their health and personal safety in the pursuit of ideal beauty. But what many of us do not realise is that the body ideals we see in films, music videos and advertisements do not necessarily reflect or celebrate the diversity of body types in the real world.

Being a teenager can be tough! It is a challenging time as your body goes through many changes and this can play havoc with your feelings. It can be a time of great stress and insecurity and it is all too easy to get caught up in worrying about your body image. Our increasing dependence on technology and exposure to social media is both a blessing and a curse, and sometimes what we see online only adds to our individual anxieties.

But it is not just the young who are worried about their appearance. Every year, around the world, thousands of people risk their health, mental well-being, relationships and financial security for the sake of beauty.

In this section, not only will we look at some of the lengths that people go to in order to conform to certain standards of beauty, but we will also explore the ways in which we can combat the negative effects of media misrepresentation.

ⓘ Did you know that in Elizabethan times, a pale complexion was considered to be a sign of nobility, wealth and delicacy? To achieve whiter skin, women in the western world would use *ceruse*, a foundation made with lead. And, yes, lead is poisonous! Some of the terrible side effects included hair loss, corrosion of the skin and muscle paralysis. It even damaged your brain.

The ancient Egyptians used bromine to dye their lips. Bromine is incredibly toxic and prolonged exposure to it can lead to respiratory and circulatory problems. It is also incredibly corrosive.

In the early 1900s, dieters in Europe who were desperate to lose weight used to swallow tapeworm cysts. The idea was that the parasites would reach maturity in the intestines and then absorb the food. And then no more fat! Just weight loss, diarrhoea and vomiting …

To find out more about tapeworm and other crazy diets, visit this website: **www.bbc.co.uk/news/magazine-20695743**

■ In Elizabethan times, women used a lead-based foundation to achieve a pale complexion

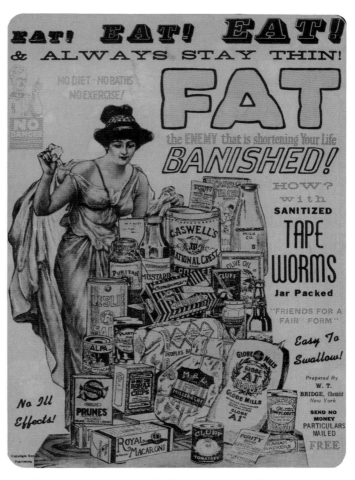

■ Men and women once believed that swallowing tapeworm parasites would help them to lose weight

■ The ancient Egyptians used bromine, an incredibly toxic substance, to stain their lips

ACTIVITY: Dark is Beautiful

In India, the skin lightening industry is worth around $450 million dollars. Every year, hundreds of men and women apply dangerous concoctions to their skin in the hope of attaining a lighter complexion. These creams and bleaching agents can have adverse side effects, but this does not stop the companies which make them from advertising them, sometimes even enlisting the help of celebrities.

To combat negative attitudes towards darker skin and to counter irresponsible advertising, the 'Dark is Beautiful' campaign was launched in 2009 by Women of Worth, a charity based in India. The campaign seeks to raise awareness of skin tone discrimination and celebrates the diversity and beauty of all skin tones. You can find out more about the campaign by visiting: http://womenofworth.in/dark-is-beautiful/

Look carefully at the Women of Worth poster on the opposite page, which features a well-known Indian actress and producer, Vishakha Singh. Then answer the following questions:

1 **Identify** the target audience for this multimodal text.
2 **Identify** the message of the poster.
3 How does the text in the poster link to the image?
4 Can you **infer** why the charity has chosen to use a celebrity to convey this message?
5 **Identify** examples of language used in the text which best convey the message. **Analyse** the words and **comment** on the effect they may have on the target audience.
6 **Identify** any visual features which help convey the message. **Analyse** and **comment** on the effect these features may have on the target audience.
7 'Stay UNfair. Stay Beautiful.' is an example of which language technique/s? What effect does it have?
8 **Evaluate** whether the designers have been successful in conveying the message of the campaign.

▼ Links to: Sciences: Biology

Melanin is the brown pigment found in our skin. It is important because it protects our bodies from the harmful effects of the Sun's ultraviolet (UV) rays.

You can find out more about the damaging effects of UV rays by watching this video about sunburn and skin cancer: **https://youtu.be/kmqhzG8QamU**

When people apply skin-bleaching agents to their skin, they slow down the rate of melanin production and make themselves more vulnerable to developing harmful skin conditions.

■ An advert promoting skin-lightening products – in many parts of the world, having lighter skin is considered to be more desirable

■ A poster for the 'Dark is Beautiful' campaign

ACTIVITY: Let's get body positive!

Read the online article on page 109 and then **discuss** the following in pairs:

1 What do you **understand** from the expression 'body positivity'?
2 Why is Megan a good spokesperson for body positivity?
3 Where do you think the 'not good enough' mentality mentioned in the article comes from? Who does Megan hold partly responsible for this?
4 **Identify** the purpose of Megan's blog.
5 **Infer** the message Megan is trying to convey and **identify** the target audience.
6 **Evaluate** Megan's rules for being body positive.
7 What do you think about body positivity as a movement? How might it benefit people of your age?
8 **Evaluate** the role that social media plays in developing our ideas about self image and beauty. Does it have a positive or negative influence? Or both?

EXTENSION: EATING DISORDERS

Megan describes herself as a 'recovered anorexic'. Eating disorders such as anorexia and bulimia are complex mental health issues which affect hundreds and thousands of people worldwide. A report commissioned by the eating disorder charity b-eat in 2015 estimated that more than 725 000 people, women and men, in the UK alone were suffering from an eating disorder.

In pairs or groups, carry out some research about eating disorders using the websites below:

www.b-eat.co.uk

http://eating-disorders.org.uk

www.mind.org.uk/information-support/types-of-mental-health-problems/eating-problems/#.WBCmGGNaHzl

Find out:
• what eating disorders are
• what can trigger an eating disorder
• who is most likely to develop an eating disorder (consider gender, age, location).

Tug of war

Many people blame media representations of men and women for causing eating disorders in young people. What is your opinion about this? As a class, consider this issue.

In groups of three, **draw** a rope on a large sheet of paper, with the two ends representing opposing views on the issue. Think about which view you have and why. Write your justifications on Post-it notes. Write down other reasons, or 'tugs', for both sides of the issue and then stick your Post-its on the rope.

Now generate some 'what if' questions for issues, factors or concerns that might need to be explored further in order to resolve the issue. Write these down and stick the Post-its above the rope.

In pairs, reflect on the activity. What new ideas do you have about media representations and eating disorders? Do you still feel the same way about it? Have you changed your mind or do you still have the same point of view?

Let's read about how one anorexia sufferer became the most body confident girl on Instagram.

From anorexic to body confident

Meet Megan, the name behind the hugely successful website www.bodyposipanda.com, the website inspiring many people suffering with eating disorders to seek help.

Megan, 22, describes herself on her website as a 'recovered anorexic' and 'recovered self-loather' who is trying her best to shatter the 'not good enough' mentality she feels we've all been taught about our bodies.

Megan's struggle with anorexia nervosa first began in 2007, when she writes she had a fleeting and intense friendship with the new girl in school.

'It was the kind of friendship you can only have in those early teenage years, desperately clinging on to each other like life rafts through the rough tides of puberty,' she says.

She writes: 'We spent every day together, drowning each other in our insecurities. Occasionally sneaking out of the house at 6am to go running, or playing badminton for hours and hours in my garden, eventually crawling inside and feeding our exhaustion with mountains of biscuits and cakes.'

She then goes on to reveal that what they were really doing was coaching each other towards the eating disorders they were both teetering on the edge of.

She didn't see the harm being done, or how toxic the friendship was. She felt relieved to have found someone else to wallow with in the 'new pits of self hatred'.

Later Megan lost touch with her former friend after she moved away. With her gone, Megan fell further into the depths of her eating disorder.

Now, years later, thanks to years of determination and willpower plus the coping mechanisms and strategies she outlines on her blog, Megan is fully recovered.

Her body confidence oozes out from the realm of her social media accounts. She has an Instagram following of 22.5k at @bodyposipanda, where she regularly posts updates of her body, comparing past and present images of herself along with positive messages that truly resonate with her audience.

The main aim of Megan's website is to take a stand against a world that profits from teaching people to hate themselves, while showing that same world that recovery is possible.

Megan has three rules for being body positive that helped with her recovery:

Change what you see

'Take the blindfold off. Take control of what you're seeing. Turn off the channels that only glorify one body type and close the pages that sell you whitewashed, one-dimensional ideals.

Fill your social media up with a plethora of perfection. Find the plus size models and the body positive activists. Find all the wonderful bodies being embraced that our media doesn't show us.

Every size, every skin colour, every age, every ability, every gender – there are all kinds of bodies out there that belong to people who are completely happy in them, exactly as they are.'

Get feminist

She feels body positivity is a feminist issue. That all genders experience body image issues and recently the expectations of unachievable, Adonis-like body standards for men are more pervasive than ever. And that it's undeniable that the prime targets for the diet and beauty industries over the years have been women (including anyone who identifies as a woman).

And lastly …

Make the commitment

And by this she doesn't mean control. She means strength, the strength to keep going. Because according to Megan, the bottom line is you deserve to feel good about your body.

By Hattie Gladwell, www.metro.co.uk, 21 September 2015

ACTIVITY: Face

Face is a novel by the British writer Benjamin Zephaniah. The story centres on the impact of a life-changing incident on a teenage boy called Martin and his group of friends. Martin is a popular and confident boy, a little vain at times, until his face becomes disfigured following a serious car crash. This incident has a huge influence on Martin's point of view on many things in his life, especially his relationships with others.

Task 1

In the extract below, Martin views his face in the mirror for the first time after the accident. Read the text and then answer the questions which follow.

> For a moment Martin held the mirror against his chest, then he slowly lifted it up until he was looking into his own eyes. He suffered a silent shock. His eyes were completely red with only minute bits of white coming through. He focused on his pupils, leaving the rest of his face temporarily out of focus. His pupils looked untouched, unmoved by the chaos around them. But even when out of focus, he could not help but see the rough unevenness of his skin. Then Martin focused his eyes on the skin on his face. It was bright red in places, and brown in others. He noticed pinky white bits, which looked like flesh with no skin cover, where he could see veins. His whole face had swollen and changed shape. His right cheek was blistered, his left cheek had swollen – the two halves of his face looked completely different from each other. The contours of his face were jagged. On seeing his lips, which were swollen as if he had been in a fight, his breath left him for a moment. He instinctively shut his eyes, then slowly opened them again. He lifted a hand up to feel his head. Much of the back and sides of his hair had survived but the top front had mostly gone, only small patches were left. Martin was scared by what he saw but could not look away.

1 **Identify** which one of the highlighted words in the text has the same meaning as 'very small' or 'tiny'.

2 Match the following words from the text to their definitions:

   a temporarily   an outline or edge
   b contour   bigger, inflated
   c instinctively   for a short or set period of time
   d swollen   without thinking

3 If something is described as 'jagged', it:
   a   is soft
   b   is a dark colour
   c   has sharp, pointy edges.
4 **Identify** two things that Martin does which show he is reluctant to look at his new face properly.
5 How do you think Martin feels after seeing his new face? Try to **understand** how he might feel and write a short paragraph. Include as many adjectives as you can to **describe** his emotions, and support your response with some quotes from the text.
6 What effect do you think a change in someone's physical appearance can have on their self-esteem? **Evaluate** how it could affect their lifestyle.

Task 2

In the novel, Martin decides to opt for an operation which will improve his physical appearance but will not make any difference to his health.

Many people now opt for cosmetic surgery and sometimes, in countries where there is a public health service, patients do not need to pay for these types of procedures themselves. Some people claim that their appearance is affecting their mental health and request to have their noses altered, their fat reduced (liposuction) or to have a 'tummy tuck' (where loose skin on the stomach is removed). There can, of course, be dangers associated with these types of procedures. What is your opinion about this? **Discuss** in pairs or groups of three.

Copy the table below and write down all the arguments you can think of for and against having cosmetic surgery. Add as many rows as you like. You may want to use Google or another search engine to carry out some research.

Arguments for cosmetic surgery	Arguments against cosmetic surgery

Now **synthesize** your arguments and write a speech either for or against cosmetic surgery. It must be between 200 and 250 words in length. You can use the *Writing to argue* box on page 112 to help you.

◆ Assessment opportunities

♦ In this activity you have practised skills that are assessed using Criterion B: Reading and Criterion D: Writing

Writing to argue

Argumentative writing is very similar to persuasive writing because you can use many of the same techniques. (To refresh your memory you may like to look back at *English for the IB MYP 1: by Concept* Chapter 5.) However, when you write to argue you must follow a very specific structure.

Follow this guide to help you plan your response:

1   Before you begin to write, you must decide which side of the argument you are on. Are you arguing for or against the chosen topic? Your position should be completely clear to you as well as to your audience or readers.

2   In your *introduction* you should make a general statement about the topic or issue you are arguing for or against. For example, 'In 2015, 51 000 Britons opted for cosmetic surgery.' You should then clearly establish which side of the argument you are on.

3   **Present** your *arguments* (for/against) in a clear and logical fashion. Include facts, statistics and anecdotes to support your arguments. Use discourse markers such as 'to begin with' or 'secondly'. You can find more examples of these on this website: **http://dictionary.cambridge.org/grammar/british-grammar/discourse-markers-so-right-okay**

4   Next, you should **demonstrate** that you have an awareness and understanding of the *other side* of the argument. This makes you seem more knowledgeable about the topic, and your audience is therefore more likely to take you seriously. You can start this section with a statement such as: 'Although there are many arguments against plastic surgery, many people believe that there are some significant benefits.'

5   *Counter argue*. You do not want to make your writing too balanced – one side of the argument has to be more dominant in an argumentative text. Use this opportunity to challenge all of the arguments you have presented in your previous paragraph to strengthen your position.

6   Finally, in your *conclusion* you should briefly **summarize** your side of the argument and end on a decisive and memorable note.

! Take action: How can I make a difference?

! Do you think the media should be held responsible for promoting unrealistic body ideals? Get writing! Write a letter to a magazine you have seen and try to persuade them to use models who reflect the true diversity of body types in the real world.

! Promote the spirit of BOPO. BOPO, or body positivity, is on the rise. Promote it in your school by encouraging people to celebrate the way they look. **Create** posters to raise each others' self esteem with positive messages such as: 'You are good enough exactly as you are' or 'Life is way too short to spend another day at war with yourself'. You can find inspiration for these online.

! Think back to the WatchCut videos you saw earlier in the chapter. Did you find a video about beauty in your home country? If not, take action and contact WatchCut to ask them to consider it for a future video.

! In the meantime, do some research about the changing fashion and beauty trends in your country. To make things easier, you might want to focus on a particular time span, for example, from 1900 to 1950 or from 1930 to the present day – the choice is yours. Perhaps you could **present** your findings as a timeline.

! Experiment with your own style. Take inspiration from those around you and get out of your comfort zone.

■ It can be fun to try out new styles – this woman is experimenting with a vintage hat

---

DISCUSS

Have your opinions on 'beauty' changed after reading this chapter?

■ 'People often say that "beauty is in the eye of the beholder," and I say that the most liberating thing about beauty is realizing that you are the beholder. This empowers us to find beauty in places where others have not dared to look, including inside ourselves.' Salma Hayek

SOME SUMMATIVE TASKS TO TRY

Use these tasks to apply and extend your learning in this chapter. These tasks are designed so that you can evaluate your learning at different levels of achievement in the Language acquisition criteria.

THIS TASK CAN BE USED TO EVALUATE YOUR LEARNING IN CRITERION C TO PROFICIENT LEVEL

Task 1: Interactive oral – the true cost of beauty

- Look again at the multimodal text on page 107. Using PowerPoint or a similar programme, prepare a presentation on skin lightening or one of the controversial beauty issues listed below:
  - ☐ Hair weaves
  - ☐ Eye enlargement surgery
  - ☐ Leg extension surgery
  - ☐ Plastic surgery
- Your presentation must be a minimum of six slides and you are expected to speak for 4–5 minutes.

Use the following questions to **organize** your research and presentation:
1. What is the beauty issue?
2. What does it involve? Are there many different methods/types?
3. Where in the world is it most common?
4. Why do people want to do it? (You may want to think about history and culture.)
5. Is it more popular for men or women, or equally popular for both?
6. What are the dangers?
7. Is it ever justified?
8. Is it worth paying such a high price for beauty?

THIS TASK CAN BE USED TO EVALUATE YOUR LEARNING IN CRITERION B
TO PROFICIENT LEVEL

Task 2: Girls Under Pressure

- Read the extract on pages 116–118 taken from *Girls Under Pressure*, a novel by Jacqueline Wilson, told from the point of view of a thirteen-year-old girl.
- Then answer the following questions, using your own words as much as possible.
- Refer as closely as possible to the text, **justifying** your answers and giving examples when required.
- Do not use translating devices or dictionaries for this task.
- You will have 60 minutes to complete this task.

1. **Identify** the name of the **narrator**. (strand i)
2. **Identify** where the extract is set. (strand i)
3. **Infer** who the target audience is for this novel. (strand ii)
4. **Interpret** how the narrator feels when she sees Magda's new jacket. (strand iii)
5. **Identify** an expression in the text which means the same as 'to have a look'. (strand i)
6. The words 'soft supple stylish leather' are an example of: (strand ii)
   a **personification**   b **simile**   c **alliteration**.
7. How do you know that the narrator wishes she was thinner? Find *two* pieces of evidence from the text (quotes) to **justify** your answer. (strands i and iii)
8. Look again at one of quotes you selected in Question 7. **Analyse** the effect of the language used by the writer. (strand ii)
9. **Interpret** the meaning of the idiom 'the penny drops'. (strands ii and iii)
10. Choose a character from the text and write about their personality. Which IB learner profile attributes do they possess? Which attributes do they lack? (strand iii)
11. What happens when the narrator gets roped into entering the modelling competition? **Interpret** how she feels. How do you think this will affect her? Refer to the text in your answer. (strands i and iii)
12. Can you relate to the characters in the text in any way? Have you ever experienced something similar? Would you act in the same way as any of the girls? (strand iii)
13. What message do you think the writer is trying to convey through the novel? (strand iii)

Magda certainly shows stylish evidence of spoiling when we meet up with her at the Flowerfields Shopping Centre entrance. She's wearing a brand new bright red furry jacket that looks wonderful.

'Is that your Christmas present, Magda?' Nadine asks.

'Of course not! No, I had a little moan to Mum that although my leather jacket is ultra hip it isn't really warm – so she had a word with Dad and we went on a little shopping trip and voilà!' She twirls round in the jacket, turning up the collar and striking poses like a fashion model.

'It looks fantastic, Magda,' I say enviously. 'Hey, what about your leather jacket then? Don't you want it any more?'

I've been longing for a leather jacket like Magda's for months. I've tried dropping hints at home. Hints!

I've made brazen pleas. To no avail. Dad and Anna won't listen. I have to put up with my boring boring boring old coat that doesn't do a thing for me. It makes me look dumpier than ever. I know it's too tight over my bum. I'd have sold my soul for Magda's soft supple stylish leather – but now her furry scarlet jacket is even better.

Nadine fiddles at Magda's neck to have a deck at the label.

'Wow! Whistles,' says Nadine. She bought her black velvet at Camden Market. It's a bit shabby and stained now, but it still looks good on her. Anything looks good on Nadine because she's so tall and thin and striking.

'Come on then, you two. Shopping time,' I say.

'Do you really want plasticine, Ellie?' Nadine asks, linking arms.

I wish I was made out of plasticine. Then I'd roll myself out, long and very very thin. I'd stretch my stubby fingers into elegant manicured hands, I'd narrow my neck and my ankles, I'd scrape huge great chunks off my bottom, I'd pull off all my brown wiry hair and make myself a new long blond hairstyle …

'Ellie?' says Nadine. 'You're dreaming.'

Yes. Dream on, Ellie.

'I don't really know what I want,' I say. 'Let's look round for a bit.'

'Shall we go and see the teddy bears?' says Magda.

There are too many people waiting for the bubble lifts so we go on the giant escalator. As we get nearer the top I start to focus. There are hundreds of teenage girls milling about up there, and big banners everywhere with the Spicy logo.

'Spicy, the magazine,' says Magda. 'Are they doing a special promotion? I hope they're giving out free goodies. Come on, you two, let's get in the queue quick.'

She dashes up the last stretch of the escalator, her patent boots shining.

'Come on, Ellie,' says Nadine, starting to run too.

'I think Spicy sucks,' I say. 'I don't really want any of their freebies.'

'Then you can use them for Christmas presents, right?' says Nadine.

So the three of us join the queue. It's so jam-packed and jostling that we have to hang on hard to each other. It's horribly hot at the top of the building. Magda unbuttons her jacket and fans her face. Nadine's ghostly pallor pinkens.

'Maybe this isn't such a great idea,' I say.

I'm squashed up so close to the girl in front of me that her long silky hair veils my face. Everyone's so much taller than me. I try craning my neck but the nearer we get to the front the harder it is to see what's going on. Lights keep on flashing and every now and then there's a squeal, but they're playing such loud rock music it's hard to hear what anyone's saying.

'Magda?' I tug her furry sleeve, but she's bouncing away to the music and doesn't respond.

'Nadine?' She's tall enough to see – and she's staring, transfixed.

'What's happening?' I yell at her.

She shouts something about a competition.

'Do we have to go in for it?' I say, sighing. I don't think I'll be any good at a Spicy competition. I don't know much about music. I don't even bother reading NME. Nadine will do much better than me.

Or maybe it's a fashion competition. I still haven't got a clue. Magda talks designer labels like they're all personal friends of hers but I don't even know how to pronounce the Italian ones, and I can never work out what all those initials stand for.

'Let's go and shop,' I beg, but there's a little surge forward, and suddenly Magda shoves hard, tugging us along after her.

We're almost at the front. I blink in the bright lights. There are huge Spicy posters and lots of promotion girls in pink T-shirts rushing round taking everyone's names and addresses. Each girl goes up in turn to a backdrop and stands there looking coy while a photographer clicks his camera.

There's a very pretty girl having her photo taken now: long hair, huge eyes, skinny little figure. She poses with one thumb hooked casually in her jeans. She pouts her lips just like a real model.

The next girl's really stunning too. I look round.

They all are. And then at long last the penny drops.

This is a modelling competition!   ➤

'Oh my God!' I gasp.

Magda darts forward and claims her turn. She takes off her jacket and slings it over one shoulder, her other hand fluffing up her bright blond hair. She smiles, her lipstick glossy, her teeth white. She looks good. She may be too small, but she looks really cute, really sexy.

'Wow, get Magda,' I say to Nadine. 'Come on, let's get out of here.'

But Nadine is still staring. I pull her. She doesn't budge.

'Nadine, please! They'll think we're going in for this model competition crap,' I say.

'Well. We might as well have a go, eh?' says Nadine.

'What?'

It'll be a laugh,' says Nadine, and she rushes forward to give her name to a girl in pink.

I watch Nadine stand in front of the camera. It's suddenly like I'm watching a stranger. I've always known Magda is seriously sexy and attractive. She looked pretty stunning at eleven that first day I sat next to her at secondary school. But I've known Nadine most of my life. She's more like my sister than my friend. I've never really looked at her.

I look at her now. She stands awkwardly, not smiling, with none of Magda's confidence. She's not really pretty. But I can see the girls in pink are taking a real interest in her, and the photographer asks her to turn while he takes several photos. Her long hair looks so black and glossy, her skin so eerily pale. She's so tall, with her slender neck and beautiful hands and long long legs. And she's so thin.

Model-girl thin.

'You're next. Name?' says a pink T-shirt, shoving a clipboard in my face.

'What? No! Not me,' I stammer, and I turn and try to elbow my way back through the huge queue.

'Watch it!'

'Hey, stop shoving.'

'What's her problem, eh?'

'Surely she doesn't think she could make it as a model? She's far too fat!'

Too fat, too fat, too fat.

Too F-A-T!

Extract from Girls Under Pressure, *by Jacqueline Wilson*

Reflection

In this chapter we have explored different **points of view** about beauty and how these ideas are conditioned by our environment and **culture**. We have explored fashion and beauty as a means of **personal expression** and learnt about the reasons behind some of the choices people make. We have also seen how fashion has evolved over time and how historical factors can have an impact on changing trends. Finally, we have evaluated some of the negative **messages** about body image that young people are bombarded with and their dangerous consequences.

Use this table to reflect on your own learning in this chapter						
Questions we asked	Answers we found	Any further questions now?				
Factual: What is fashion?						
Conceptual: Does it matter what we look like? How can we express ourselves through the way we look? How does the way we dress reflect who we are? How have our notions of beauty changed over time?						
Debatable: What is beauty? To what extent is our idea of true beauty influenced by our environment? Can the pursuit of ideal beauty be dangerous? What price are we willing to pay for ideal beauty?						
Approaches to learning you used in this chapter:	Description – what new skills did you learn?	How well did you master the skills?				
		Novice	Learner	Practitioner	Expert	
Communication skills						
Collaboration skills						
Affective skills						
Information literacy skills						
Learner profile attribute(s)	Reflect on the importance of being balanced for your learning in this chapter.					
Balanced						

(6) What's your story?

○ The **conventions** of story writing not only allow writers to express their **creativity**, but also give them a **voice** through which they can express a certain **point of view** and create **empathy** for others. The act of reading and sharing stories can help us better understand our **orientation in space and time**.

CONSIDER THESE QUESTIONS:

Factual: What is a story? What are the typical conventions of storytelling?

Conceptual: Why do we tell stories? What can we learn from stories? What makes a good story?

Debatable: Do stories matter? Do life stories matter? What can we gain from reading personal narratives?

Now **share and compare** your thoughts and ideas with your partner, or with the whole class.

■ We all have a story to tell – we just need to know how to bring it to life!

┌○ IN THIS CHAPTER, WE WILL ...

■ **Find out** what a story is and learn about the typical conventions of story writing.

■ **Explore** the reasons why people write and what we can gain from telling stories.

■ **Take action** to encourage others to read, write and share stories.

■ These Approaches to Learning (ATL) skills will be useful …

- Creative-thinking skills
- Critical-thinking skills
- Information literacy skills
- Transfer skills
- Communication skills
- Collaboration skills

● We will reflect on this learner profile attribute …

- Open-minded – we critically appreciate our own cultures and personal histories, as well as the values and traditions of others. We seek and evaluate a range of points of view, and we are willing to grow from the experience.

◆ Assessment opportunities in this chapter:

- Criterion A: Listening
- Criterion B: Reading
- Criterion C: Speaking
- Criterion D: Writing

KEY WORDS

character	non-fiction
embedded narrative	pseudonym
fiction	setting
memoir	

ACTIVITY: Build a story

■ ATL

- Creative-thinking skills: Make unexpected or unusual connections between objects and/or ideas

You are going to work in a group to build a story.

First, on your own, write a sentence on a Post-it note. It can be about anything you like. Do not share your sentence with anyone else and fold it in half so it cannot be read. Make sure that everyone in the group has done the same.

Place all your folded Post-it notes in a box and mix them up.

Arrange yourselves in a circle. One person should pick out a Post-it note from the box and read it out loud. This will be the first line of the story you are going to **create** together.

The person sitting on the right of the first person should add the next sentence to the story, and so on. Each student must ensure that they use the appropriate tense and that their contribution links well to the previous sentence to help drive the story forward.

Ask your teacher or another student to write down the sentences so you have a record of the story. Then make photocopies.

In pairs, proofread your story. Give each other feedback on the contribution you made to the overall story. **Identify** the elements that make a good story and make one or two suggestions on how it could be improved.

◆ Assessment opportunities

- In this activity you have practised skills that are assessed using Criterion C: Speaking

What is a story?

DO STORIES MATTER?

■ What does it take to write a good story?

We all have a story to tell and all of these stories matter. Defined simply, a *story* is an account of imaginary or real people, told or written, and shared for the purpose of entertaining others. But stories are much more than just a form of entertainment.

Stories have the power to transport us into other worlds. They help us to gain a better understanding of others and teach us **empathy**. Stories give us a voice and allow us to share our personal experiences, preserve our traditions and pass on knowledge. They can be shared in many, many different ways. We can tell stories through prose, pictures, poems, songs and films.

The one thing which all stories have in common, however, is the magic they can bring to our lives. Stories have the power to influence the way we think and feel about the world. They provide us with an opportunity to escape temporarily from our lives, and to step into someone else's shoes so that we can see things from another point of view.

Without stories, life would not be the same, and in this chapter we will explore how and why stories matter.

ACTIVITY: What is the most important element of a good story?

We are all different, so it is only natural that we all have different ideas about what makes a good story a *great* story. But maybe there are some things which we can all agree on.

Watch this short video of some writers, journalists and film producers talking about what they believe are the most important elements of a good story, and then answer the questions which follow: www.theatlantic.com/video/index/374941/what-makes-a-story-great/

1 **Identify** and **list** the elements mentioned in the video.
2 **Discuss** these elements in pairs or groups and decide whether or not you agree with the speakers in the video.
3 What point is made about audience?
4 **Identify** the simile that the final speaker uses to express his point about storytelling. What does he mean? Do you agree?
5 In pairs or groups, **discuss** what you think makes a good story. Can you add to the list that you compiled in Question 1?

DISCUSS

What are some of your favourite stories? Why do you like them so much?

Can you **identify** any features of the stories that make them so enjoyable or memorable?

■ Do you have a favourite story?

What are the typical conventions of storytelling?

WHAT MAKES A GOOD STORY?

Stories come in all shapes and sizes. A story can be long and fill an entire novel, or a story can be short and consist of less than a thousand words. Stories can be **fictional**, and describe imaginary people, events or places, or they can be **non-fictional**, and be based on true events, people or places.

But like all texts, stories must follow certain conventions in order to be considered as such. These conventions enable writers to effectively produce structured narratives and help them to achieve their purpose. But how do we judge whether a story is a good story?

Readers want to immerse themselves in the world that has been conjured up by the writer's pen. They want to laugh, cry and fall in love with convincing, three-dimensional characters they can relate to. They want to travel to faraway lands without leaving the comfort of their armchairs. But most of all, readers want to be entertained.

A storyteller's purpose is to engage his or her readers through detail, description and **dialogue**. It is the storyteller's job to take their readers on a journey through the worlds they have created, so it is essential that these stories follow a logical, coherent structure – a lost or frustrated reader is not a happy reader!

In this section we will look more closely at the conventions of story-writing and learn how we can use detail and description to enrich our own writing.

ACTIVITY: What makes a story a story?

■ ATL

- Information literacy skills: Access information to be informed and inform others

A story can be fact, fiction or sometimes a blend of the two. There are, however, some elements that remain the same, whether the events in the story have been created by the author's imagination or are rooted in reality.

Copy the table below. Use Google or another search engine to find definitions for these typical conventions of a story and complete the middle column.

Convention	Definition	Example: (book title)
Plot		
Narrative		
Narrator		
Setting		
Characters		
Genre		

In pairs or groups, **discuss** the last story you read or your favourite story, if you have one. **Describe** what the story was about and **evaluate** why you did or did not like it.

Fill in the final column of the table using your chosen story as an example.

◆ Assessment opportunities

- ◆ In this activity you have practised skills that are assessed using Criterion C: Speaking

Point of view

All narratives are told from a particular *point of view*. We refer to this as the story's *narrative voice* and there are two main categories – **first person narrative** and **third person narrative**.

In first person narratives, the story is told from the viewpoint of a character who speaks or writes using first person pronouns such as 'I' or 'we'.

In third person narratives, the story is told using third person pronouns such as 'he', 'she', 'it' or 'they'.

ACTIVITY: Who is telling the story?

 ATL

- Communication skills: Read critically and for comprehension
- Critical-thinking skills: Evaluate evidence or arguments

In pairs or groups of three, read the two extracts below, taken from the openings of two novels, and then answer the questions which follow:

> My name is Mary Katherine Blackwood. I am eighteen years old, and I live with my sister Constance. I have often thought that with any luck at all I could have been born a werewolf, because the two middle fingers on both my hands are the same length, but I have had to be content with what I had. I dislike washing myself, and dogs, and noise. I like my sister Constance, and Richard Plantagenet, and Amanita phalloides, the death-cup mushroom. Everyone else in my family is dead.

From *We Have Always Lived in the Castle* by Shirley Jackson

> The boy with fair hair lowered himself down the last few feet of rock and began to pick his way towards the lagoon. Though he had taken off his school sweater and trailed it now from one hand, his grey shirt stuck to him and his hair was plastered to his forehead.

> All round him the long scar smashed into the jungle was a bath of heat. He was clambering heavily among the creepers and broken trunks when a bird, a vision of red and yellow, flashed upwards with a witch-like cry; and this cry was echoed by another.

From *Lord of the Flies* by William Golding

1 **Identify** which narrative voice is used in each text.
2 **Evaluate** which narrative voice is better for establishing a sense of character.
3 **Evaluate** which narrative voice is better for establishing a setting.
4 What are the advantages and disadvantages of a first person narrative?
5 What are the advantages and disadvantages of a third person narrative?
6 Which narrative voice do you prefer, first or third? **Explain** why.
7 Make a list of books you have read and see if you can remember which are written in the first person and which are in the third person.

◆ Assessment opportunities

- ◆ In this activity you have practised skills that are assessed using Criterion B: Reading

ACTIVITY: Bringing a story to life

■ ATL

- Transfer skills: Apply skills and knowledge in unfamiliar situations
- Communication skills: Give and receive meaningful feedback
- Creative-thinking skills: Create original works and ideas; Use existing works and ideas in new ways

One of the most magical things about storytellers is that they have the power to transport us to places and times distant from our own. They achieve this by using specific language and **stylistic devices** in order to stimulate our imaginations and bring these worlds to life.

Vivid descriptions of places and people, authentic sounding dialogue and a variety of sentence lengths all help to draw the reader into a story.

Task 1

To begin, let's remind ourselves of some of the stylistic devices we can use to make our writing richer. To do this, copy and complete the table below. If you get stuck, you can work with a partner.

Stylistic device	Example	Definition
Alliteration		
Simile		Comparing things using 'like' or 'as … as'
Metaphor	Her eyes were emeralds glinting in the fading light.	
Personification		Giving an object human characteristics
Onomatopoeia	Splash! Buzz! Pop!	

Task 2

Now let's see if we can make some magic of our own!

Look at the opening sentences of a story opposite. Rewrite it to add more detailed descriptions and include as many of the stylistic devices from the table as you can.

Swap your rewritten passage with a partner. Use a highlighter pen on each other's passage to **identify** examples of interesting language and stylistic devices.

Compare your new versions to the original passage and **evaluate** whether the text has been improved.

Why not include some onomatopoeia here to capture the shrill sound of the alarm?

Try replacing the highlighted words with more interesting verbs, or adding some adverbs to make the passage more animated. Use a thesaurus to help you.

Let's add some personification here. Try adding a **reporting verb** to bring the bed to life.

My alarm clock rang. It was time to get ready for school. I stretched my arms and then got out of bed. The mattress made a funny noise as I got up. I walked over to my cupboard and took out my school uniform. I laid it down on the bed and stared at it for a while.

Here is an opportunity to add some detail. **Describe** the school uniform in more depth. Think about the colours, the textures of the fabrics and what exactly it consists of. Is it brand new? Or has it been handed down from an older sibling? Think carefully about your choice of adjectives.

At the moment, we do not know very much at all about how the person in the story is feeling. By changing some of the verbs, and by adding adverbs and adjectives, you can alter the mood of the text. For example, verbs like *leaped*, *jumped* or *skipped* convey a positive tone, and suggest that the person is excited about the day ahead. Alternatively, the person might be dreading their day at school, in which case using verbs like *dragged* or *forced*, and adverbs such as *reluctantly*, might be more appropriate.

Task 3

In pairs, complete the following tasks:

1 **Give the story a provisional title. You can always change it later.**
2 **Create a plan for the story. Decide on the following aspects:**
   - **Genre: What kind of story is it going to turn into?**
   - **Plot: What is going to happen? You have a beginning which you need to extend. Decide on the middle and the end. It might be useful to create a storyboard to help you plan this.**
   - **Narrative voice: So far the story has been told in the first person. Do you want to keep it in the first person or change it to the third person? (If you change to the third person, you will have to rewrite the beginning.)**
   - **Setting: Where and when is your story going to be set?**
   - **Characters: Who is your main character? How many other key characters are there going to be?**
3 **Once you are happy with your plan, have a go at writing the second and third paragraphs of your story. Remember to include as many stylistic devices as you can.**

◆ Assessment opportunities

◆ In this activity you have practised skills that are assessed using Criterion D: Writing

Dialogue

Dialogue is a conversation between two or more people in a story. Good, authentic sounding dialogue can make your story more engaging and is a great way to give your characters a voice.

Punctuating dialogue and embedding it appropriately can be a little tricky. Have a look at the rules below to help you get it right.

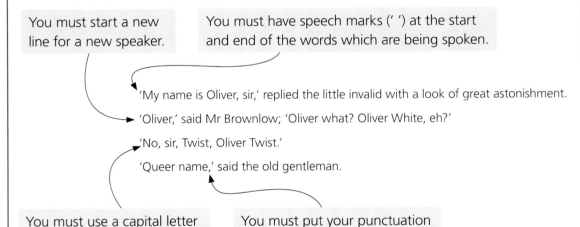

You must start a new line for a new speaker.

You must have speech marks (' ') at the start and end of the words which are being spoken.

'My name is Oliver, sir,' replied the little invalid with a look of great astonishment.

'Oliver,' said Mr Brownlow; 'Oliver what? Oliver White, eh?'

'No, sir, Twist, Oliver Twist.'

'Queer name,' said the old gentleman.

You must use a capital letter at the start of the dialogue.

You must put your punctuation inside the speech marks.

ACTIVITY: Dialogue

Now have a go at punctuating the passage below.

```
What is your name the woman asked. Pierre I said. She
narrowed her eyes and regarded me suspiciously. I suppose
you can stay here for tonight. Tomorrow we will have to
see about finding you somewhere more permanent.
```

Look back at the opening of the story you wrote on page 126. See if you can include some dialogue.

ACTIVITY: The Storyteller

■ ATL

■ Communication skills: Read critically and for comprehension

A short story is a complete narrative which a person *should* be able to read in one sitting.

'The Storyteller' is a short story by the British writer H.H. Munro, who is better known by his pseudonym (or pen name) Saki.

■ H.H. Munro

Read the story on pages 130–133 and then answer the questions below. You may use a dictionary to help you.

1 Where is the story set and in which season? **Identify** examples of language used by Saki to establish the setting.
2 Who are the characters in the story?

3 In 'The Storyteller' we find a story within a story. This is known as an embedded narrative. **Identify** and **list** – as bullet points – the key plot points which make up the *two* different narratives in the story.
4 In the opening paragraph, what does the narrator compare the children to? What does this reveal about the narrator's attitude towards the children?
5 **Identify** some of the adverbs Saki uses to convey information about some of the characters in the story. What do these adverbs tell us?
6 How is humour used in the story?
7 Which IB learner profile attributes do the children possess? Make sure you can **justify** your answer using quotes from the story.
8 How does Saki develop the character of the storyteller? Find some examples from the story to support your answer.
9 How do the children react to their aunt's story?
10 What word used by the storyteller near the start of his story captures the children's interest? **Explain** why it does this.
11 What other language and stylistic choices does the storyteller make to engage the children?
12 **Identify** and **summarize** the message of the storyteller's narrative.
13 In pairs, **discuss** the story and **evaluate** whether or not the story is a success. If it is a success, decide which elements make it successful. Can you make any links with the video you watched earlier (page 123)?
14 Do you agree with the aunt's point of view that the story was inappropriate for young children? Make sure you can **justify** your answer.

◆ Assessment opportunities

◆ In this activity you have practised skills that are assessed using Criterion B: Reading

It was a hot afternoon, and the railway carriage was correspondingly sultry, and the next stop was at Templecombe, nearly an hour ahead. The occupants of the carriage were a small girl, and a smaller girl, and a small boy. An aunt belonging to the children occupied one corner seat, and the further corner seat on the opposite side was occupied by a bachelor who was a stranger to their party, but the small girls and the small boy emphatically occupied the compartment. Both the aunt and the children were conversational in a limited, persistent way, reminding one of the attentions of a housefly that refuses to be discouraged. Most of the aunt's remarks seemed to begin with 'Don't,' and nearly all of the children's remarks began with 'Why?' The bachelor said nothing out loud. 'Don't, Cyril, don't,' exclaimed the aunt, as the small boy began smacking the cushions of the seat, producing a cloud of dust at each blow.

'Come and look out of the window,' she added.

The child moved reluctantly to the window. 'Why are those sheep being driven out of that field?' he asked.

'I expect they are being driven to another field where there is more grass,' said the aunt weakly.

'But there is lots of grass in that field,' protested the boy, 'there's nothing else but grass there. Aunt, there's lots of grass in that field.'

'Perhaps the grass in the other field is better,' suggested the aunt fatuously.

'Why is it better?' came the swift, inevitable question.

'Oh, look at those cows!' exclaimed the aunt. Nearly every field along the line had contained cows or bullocks, but she spoke as though she were drawing attention to a rarity.

'Why is the grass in the other field better?' persisted Cyril.

The frown on the bachelor's face was deepening to a scowl. He was a hard, unsympathetic man, the aunt decided in her mind. She was utterly unable to come to any satisfactory decision about the grass in the other field.

The smaller girl created a diversion by beginning to recite 'On the Road to Mandalay'. She only knew the first line, but she put her limited knowledge to the fullest possible use. She repeated the line over and over again in a dreamy but resolute and very audible voice; it seemed to the bachelor as though someone had had a bet with her that she could not repeat the line aloud two thousand times without stopping. Whoever it was who had made the wager was likely to lose his bet.

'Come over here and listen to a story,' said the aunt, when the bachelor had looked twice at her and once at the communication cord.

The children moved listlessly towards the aunt's end of the carriage. Evidently her reputation as a storyteller did not rank high in their estimation.

In a low, confidential voice, interrupted at frequent intervals by loud, petulant questionings from her listeners, she began an unenterprising and deplorably uninteresting story about a little girl who was good, and made friends with everyone on account of her goodness, and was finally saved from a mad bull by a number of rescuers who admired her moral character.

'Wouldn't they have saved her if she hadn't been good?' demanded the bigger of the small girls. It was exactly the question that the bachelor had wanted to ask.

'Well, yes,' admitted the aunt lamely, 'but I don't think they would have run quite so fast to her help if they had not liked her so much.'

'It's the stupidest story I've ever heard,' said the bigger of the small girls, with immense conviction.

'I didn't listen after the first bit, it was so stupid,' said Cyril.

The smaller girl made no actual comment on the story, but she had long ago recommenced a murmured repetition of her favourite line.

'You don't seem to be a success as a storyteller,' said the bachelor suddenly from his corner.

The aunt bristled in instant defence at this unexpected attack.

'It's a very difficult thing to tell stories that children can both understand and appreciate,' she said stiffly.

'I don't agree with you,' said the bachelor.

'Perhaps you would like to tell them a story,' was the aunt's retort.

'Tell us a story,' demanded the bigger of the small girls.

'Once upon a time,' began the bachelor, 'there was a little girl called Bertha, who was extraordinarily good.'

The children's momentarily-aroused interest began at once to flicker; all stories seemed dreadfully alike, no matter who told them.

'She did all that she was told, she was always truthful, she kept her clothes clean, ate milk puddings as though they were jam tarts, learned her lessons perfectly, and was polite in her manners.'

'Was she pretty?' asked the bigger of the small girls.

'Not as pretty as any of you,' said the bachelor, 'but she was horribly good.'

There was a wave of reaction in favour of the story; the word horrible in connection with goodness was a novelty that commended itself. It seemed to introduce a ring of truth that was absent from the aunt's tales of infant life.

'She was so good,' continued the bachelor, 'that she won several medals for goodness, which she always wore, pinned onto her dress. There was a medal for obedience, another medal for punctuality, and a third for good behaviour. They were large metal medals and they clicked against one another as she walked. No other child in the town where she lived had as many as three medals, so everybody knew that she must be an extra good child.'

➤

'Horribly good,' quoted Cyril.

'Everybody talked about her goodness, and the Prince of the country got to hear about it, and he said that as she was so very good she might be allowed once a week to walk in his park, which was just outside the town. It was a beautiful park, and no children were ever allowed in it, so it was a great honour for Bertha to be allowed to go there.'

'Were there any sheep in the park?' demanded Cyril.

'No,' said the bachelor, 'there were no sheep.'

'Why weren't there any sheep?' came the inevitable question arising out of that answer.

The aunt permitted herself a smile, which might almost have been described as a grin.

'There were no sheep in the park,' said the bachelor, 'because the Prince's mother had once had a dream that her son would either be killed by a sheep or else by a clock falling on him. For that reason the Prince never kept a sheep in his park or a clock in his palace.'

The aunt suppressed a gasp of admiration.

'Was the Prince killed by a sheep or by a clock?' asked Cyril.

'He is still alive, so we can't tell whether the dream will come true,' said the bachelor unconcernedly, 'anyway, there were no sheep in the park, but there were lots of little pigs running all over the place.'

'What colour were they?'

'Black with white faces, white with black spots, black all over, grey with white patches, and some were white all over.'

The storyteller paused to let a full idea of the park's treasures sink into the children's imaginations; then he resumed:

'Bertha was rather sorry to find that there were no flowers in the park. She had promised her aunts, with tears in her eyes, that she would not pick any of the kind Prince's flowers, and she had meant to keep her promise, so of course it made her feel silly to find that there were no flowers to pick.'

'Why weren't there any flowers?'

'Because the pigs had eaten them all,' said the bachelor promptly. 'The gardeners had told the Prince that you couldn't have pigs and flowers, so he decided to have pigs and no flowers.'

There was a murmur of approval at the excellence of the Prince's decision; so many people would have decided the other way.

'There were lots of other delightful things in the park. There were ponds with gold and blue and green fish in them, and trees with beautiful parrots that said clever things at a moment's notice, and hummingbirds that hummed all the popular tunes of the day. Bertha walked up and down and enjoyed herself immensely, and thought to herself:

"If I were not so extraordinarily good I should not have been allowed to come into this beautiful park and enjoy all that there is to be seen in it," and her three medals clinked against one another as she walked and helped to remind her how very good she really was. Just then an enormous wolf came prowling into the park to see if it could catch a fat little pig for its supper.'

'What colour was it?' asked the children, amid an immediate quickening of interest.

'Mud-colour all over, with a black tongue and pale grey eyes that gleamed with unspeakable ferocity. The first thing that it saw in the park was Bertha; her pinafore was so spotlessly white and clean that it could be seen from a great distance. Bertha saw the wolf and saw that it was stealing towards her, and she began to wish that she had never been allowed to come into the park. She ran as hard as she could, and the wolf came after her with huge leaps and bounds. She managed to reach a shrubbery of myrtle bushes and she hid herself in one of the thickest of the bushes. The wolf came sniffing among the branches, its black tongue lolling out of its mouth and its pale grey eyes glaring with rage. Bertha was terribly frightened, and thought to herself: "If I had not been so extraordinarily good I should have been safe in the town at this moment." However, the scent of the myrtle was so strong that the wolf could not sniff out where Bertha was hiding, and the bushes were so thick that he might have hunted about in them for a long time without catching sight of her, so he thought he might as well go off and catch a little pig instead. Bertha was trembling very much at having the wolf prowling and sniffing so near her, and as she trembled the medal for obedience clinked against the medals for good conduct and punctuality. The wolf was just moving away when he heard the sound of the medals clinking and stopped to listen; they clinked again in a bush quite near him. He dashed into the bush, his pale grey eyes gleaming with ferocity and triumph, and dragged Bertha out and devoured her to the last morsel. All that was left of her were her shoes, bits of clothing, and the three medals for goodness.'

'Were any of the little pigs killed?'

'No, they all escaped.'

'The story began badly,' said the smaller of the small girls, 'but it had a beautiful ending.'

'It is the most beautiful story that I ever heard,' said the bigger of the small girls, with immense decision.

'It is the only beautiful story I have ever heard,' said Cyril.

A dissentient opinion came from the aunt.

'A most improper story to tell to young children! You have undermined the effect of years of careful teaching.'

'At any rate,' said the bachelor, collecting his belongings preparatory to leaving the carriage, 'I kept them quiet for ten minutes, which was more than you were able to do.'

'Unhappy woman!' he observed to himself as he walked down the platform of Templecombe station. 'For the next six months or so those children will assail her in public with demands for an improper story!'

'The Storyteller' by H.H. Munro (Saki)

■ *A Thousand and One Nights*

ⓘ Did you know that Scheherazade is one of the most famous fictional storytellers in literature?

A Thousand and One Nights, or *The Arabian Nights* as it is commonly known, is a collection of a thousand and one stories from the Middle East, South and Central Asia and North Africa. The stories were originally shared orally and eventually recorded in Arabic. The book has had a profound influence on European art, literature and culture ever since the eighteenth and nineteenth centuries when it was first translated into French and English.

Like Saki's short story 'The Storyteller', *A Thousand and One Nights* contains an embedded narrative – in fact, it contains a thousand and one embedded narratives! You may have come across some of the stories from the collection already: 'Aladdin and the Magic Lamp', 'Ali Baba and the Forty Thieves' and 'Sinbad the Sailor' are just a few examples.

In the frame story (the main story in which all the others are embedded), Sultan Shahryar marries a girl every day, only to execute her the next morning. Resourceful Scheherazade is the only wife who manages to survive. Each night she entertains Shahryar with a new story, but deliberately withholds the ending so that he has to wait until the next night to find out what happens. She manages to do this for a thousand and one nights, and the Sultan finally falls in love with her and makes her his queen.

You can read some of the stories from the collection on this website: **www.bartleby.com/16/**

■ 'Aladdin and the Magic Lamp'

■ 'Ali Baba and the Forty Thieves'

■ 'Sinbad the Sailor'

EXTENSION: FLASH FICTION

Really, really short stories are known as *flash fiction*. But just how long should a really, really short story be? While there is no single, defined word count, most people agree that a work of flash fiction should not exceed 1000 words. Some examples of flash fiction consist of only 300 words. Some even less!

It can be tricky to develop a story with so few words at your disposal, and you might have to break some of the rules we have considered in this chapter so far. But the flash fiction writer

David Gaffney has some tips that can help. Visit the following website to read his advice: www.theguardian.com/books/2012/may/14/how-to-write-flash-fiction

Now have a go at writing your own flash fiction.

> **Hint**
>
> Stuck? Use some of the sentences on the Post-it notes from the Activity on page 121!

Why do we tell stories?

Humans are natural storytellers and for centuries we have used narratives to help us make sense of our world. Stories exist in all cultures, come in a variety of forms and, most significantly, have the power to transgress the boundaries of space and time.

By sharing stories, whether through painting images on cave walls or telling tales around a campfire, we are able to make connections with others. Stories give us a voice through which we can transmit our personal narratives, and act as a means through which we can exchange our points of view, subsequently allowing us to develop a better understanding of others.

Stories are inextricably linked to the cultures from which they originate and we can use them to maintain connections with where we are from. Stories can be a way of preserving ideas and traditions which might otherwise be lost or forgotten.

Stories have always been central to human existence and, although the ways in which we tell stories have changed over time, and will continue to do so, we will always have a need for them.

■ Telling stories to your friends can be fun

ACTIVITY: Why Your Story Matters

■ **ATL**

■ Communication skills: Read critically and for comprehension

Read Flynn Coleman's blog post for *The Huffington Post* on pages 138–139 and then answer the questions below.

1 **What does the writer say that stories allow us to do?**
2 **Why are stories powerful? Find at least *three* reasons given in the text.**
3 **What do the examples in paragraph 3 suggest about the nature of storytelling and the form that stories can take?**
4 **What do you think the writer means when she says 'today's information-saturated landscape'?**
5 **According to the text, what qualities does a good writer need to have? Can you relate these characteristics to the IB learner profile?**
6 **What stylistic device does the writer use to talk about the relationship between storytellers and the audience? Is it:**
   a **a metaphor**
   b **personification**
   c **a simile?**

■ Cave paintings were an early form of telling and recording stories

7 What is the effect of this stylistic device?
8 According to the text, what factors can stop people from sharing their stories?
9 Why does the writer use imperative sentences in paragraph 13? What does this reveal about the purpose of the text?
10 How does the writer achieve a conversational tone? Find some examples to support your answer.
11 **Summarize** the overall message of the blog.
12 The writer talks about mindfulness in the text. What is *mindfulness*? Use an online dictionary and thesaurus to find synonyms and/or phrases for mindfulness. **Create** a word cloud with the synonyms and/or phrases that you find.
13 How do you say mindfulness in your language? **Discuss** with a partner and then use Google or another search engine to find out more. Can you think of your own examples of how to be mindful at school?

◆ Assessment opportunities

◆ In this activity you have practised skills that are assessed using Criterion B: Reading

ACTIVITY: Storytellers on storytelling

■ ATL

■ Information literacy skills: Collect and analyse data
■ Collaboration skills: Listen actively to other perspectives and ideas

Flynn Coleman began her blog post with a quote from E.M. Forster, an English novelist who wrote in the early twentieth century:

'Only connect … Live in fragments no longer.' – E.M. Forster

In pairs, **interpret** what the E.M. Forster quote means. **Analyse** the thoughts, feelings, ideas or attitudes about language that are being expressed.

Now, on your own, use Google or another search engine to find out what other writers have said about storytelling. Search for some quotes about stories or storytelling from famous authors.

Share your findings with a partner or group and **interpret** and **analyse** the quotes together. Can you decide on a favourite quote? Make sure you can **explain** why you like it the best.

◆ Assessment opportunities

◆ In this activity you have practised skills that are assessed using Criterion B: Reading and Criterion C: Speaking

So far in this chapter we have learnt what stories are and about story-writing conventions. We have also seen how writers make certain language and stylistic choices to make their writing richer and to engage their audiences. We have considered what elements make a story a good story, and have attempted to plot and write our own stories. In addition, we have explored some of the reasons people have for writing and sharing stories.

Only Connect: Why Your Story Matters

'Only connect … Live in fragments no longer.' – E.M. Forster

Storytelling is as old as humanity. Our earliest ancestors told stories in pictures on the walls of caves. This same impulse has guided us across millennia. Stories make us human. They allow us to connect with our world and with ourselves, bringing meaning to our lives. In this sense, storytelling is a form of mindfulness. As a lawyer, writer, book lover, social entrepreneur, mindfulness consultant and yoga teacher, I spend much of my life immersed in stories. And I bet you do, too.

Why are stories so powerful? Well, they are more memorable than facts. Our brains are wired to respond to stories. Metaphors and anecdotes help us relate ideas to our own experiences, providing richness and texture. Stories bring you and your listeners into a multi-dimensional world, full of colors, sights, smells and emotions, making us feel as though we are actually living the story.

The greatest stories weave together symbols of our common humanity and our deepest-held values. Martin Luther King, Jr. didn't just have a few ideas about civil rights. He had a *dream*, which he shared in the form of a story. He asked listeners to participate in his vision of a more just world. John Lennon did the same. He didn't just give his point of view; he invited us to *imagine* it with him. These bold images continue to resonate and inspire.

In today's information-saturated landscape, one of the most valuable skills you can acquire is the ability to tell stories. If you want to be a good storyteller, practise listening to others. A crucial part of good storytelling is empathy: the ability to perceive and intuit what others are experiencing, and then to forge a connection on that basis.

Storytelling allows us to be present with our experience, and to draw others into that experience as well. Ever told a child a story? Laugh or light up your eyes at Dr. Seuss? Or remember way back when you were a kid, and how excited you were to tell your parents about your hand-crafted macaroni necklace, or to tell your friend about your sweet new tricycle? (Side note: was I the only one who bawled her eyes out at the end of *Where the Red Fern Grows*?)

To impact others, you must first discover what impacts you. To truly tell your story, you need to find it. That's how mindfulness can help. Visualization is a transformational way to tap into the vividness of our creative storytelling. It's proven to be one of the most powerful parts of my seminars.

Collaboration is a key part of storytelling. It's a dance between the storytellers and the audience. It's how every Pixar story gets made: people who trust each other, playing off each other's ideas and not being afraid to brainstorm. Creativity requires trust and courage, which mindfulness can help us find within ourselves.

My experience as a human rights attorney, teacher and a human being always leads back to the same conclusion: we yearn to tell our stories, and to be seen for who we are and what we have survived.

But to accept and then tell your authentic story, you need to commit to your own vulnerability, which is actually the origin of your greatest power. Brené Brown, a visionary of this work, has found through her research that:

'Owning our story can be hard but not nearly as difficult as spending our lives running from it. Embracing our vulnerabilities is risky but not nearly as dangerous as giving up on love and belonging and joy – the experiences that make us the most vulnerable. Only when we are brave enough to explore the darkness will we discover the infinite power of our light.'

We hide our stories when we feel exposed or ashamed, or when we convince ourselves that we have to be perfect. Newsflash: perfect is out. What's in? Honest self-expression. Allowing ourselves to share emotions. To be seen. To feel vulnerable. To stay open to others and to ourselves.

We're all imperfect, yet we're all worthy, just as we are. It's beautiful and worth telling. Vulnerability is also the path to our greatest creativity, courage, love, transformation, and connection. It leads us to our purpose, passion and our place in this world. It's how we shine, and how we show others they can shine, too.

So don't diminish your story. Don't hide it. Let someone see it. Let it be your strength and your evidence of bravery when you are feeling lost or beaten. Realize that, no matter who we are or what has happened in our lives, our lows, our disappointments and our struggles can be the most compelling parts of our stories. People will rally around you and you will find love and connection in the process.

If you allow it, your wounds can become the source of your greatest gifts.

It just takes a shifting of your mindset so you can see the big picture. Mindfulness helps us to achieve these radical shifts by helping us to have compassion for ourselves and others, and by giving us the confidence to live our stories to the fullest.

This is a central tenet of my creativity teaching and what often fires up my students the most. The world becomes a better place when we share ourselves with others, letting them into our story. We might discover that we have something in common with someone we once saw as different, or that our vulnerabilities help others to overcome their own fears.

Try this: take a few minutes to write five of your deepest held values. For each one, think about the experiences that have shaped this core value. Translate those experiences into stories. The next time people ask why you're taking a risk or embarking on a challenge, answer openly, honestly and with empathy. Remember, what that other person really wants to hear – what all of us really want to hear – is your story.

By Flynn Coleman, 23 June 2013, The Huffington Post

What can we learn from stories?

We tell stories all day long. Repeating something that a friend told you earlier in the day, sharing some gossip or describing an event are all narratives of a kind. It is how we are programmed to think and act. This is why stories are a great way for us to learn about new things.

Because of the way our brains function, sharing information in narrative form helps us to process complex concepts more easily. Scientists now believe that stories can help us to remember and retain facts more easily and for longer. You might want to bear this in mind next time you are revising for an exam!

Many stories, including myths, legends, folktales and fables, conceal important lessons which give us a valuable insight into human nature. Stories of this kind are often shared orally and passed down from one generation to the next. Use Google or another search engine to find out more about these types of stories.

■ Fables such as 'The Hare and the Tortoise' contain valuable lessons

ACTIVITY: Sacred stories

■ **ATL**

■ Communication skills: Make inferences and draw conclusions

Sacred stories are stories which are connected to a faith or religion. Some sacred stories originate from sacred texts such as the Torah or the Qu'ran. Others are told by followers of a faith and document the lives of key religious figures such as Gautama Buddha or Jesus Christ.

Task 1

Visit this British Library website to read some sacred stories: **www.bl.uk/learning/cult/sacred/stories/**

Click on the book with the golden cover to see some stories from the Buddhist faith. Select the story entitled 'The Elephant and the Blind Men' and watch the short video. Try to watch it without using the subtitles at first. Then answer the following questions:

1 Which IB learner profile attributes does the wise man in the story possess? Give some examples from the video.

2 The word *din* in the context of the story means:
   a a calm and quiet atmosphere
   b a loud, confused noise
   c a specific location in a jungle or forest
   d a meal eaten at a certain time of day.

3 Why did it take the wise man some time to reach the blind men?
4 What error are the blind men in the story making?
5 What is the purpose of the story?
6 What is the message of the story?

Hint

After watching the video, you can click on the 'More information' tab in the top right-hand corner to find out more.

Task 2

Now, in pairs or groups, **discuss** the following:
- **Why do people share sacred stories?**
- **Can a story that was written many years ago still help people to deal with their lives today? If so, how?**
- **In what ways do sacred stories influence lives today?**
- **Are you or your family religious? Are you familiar with any sacred stories? If so, share them with your classmates.**

◆ Assessment opportunities

◆ In this activity you have practised skills that are assessed using Criterion A: Listening and Criterion C: Speaking

■ 'The Elephant and the Blind Men'

Do life stories matter?

WHAT CAN WE GAIN FROM READING PERSONAL NARRATIVES?

Without stories, we would not have history – in fact the word *story* originates from the Latin word *historia*. Stories which record memories and personal experiences are examples of *life writing*. These individual narratives are important because they provide the human element to history. The stories reflect the individual points of view of people who lived during certain periods in time. Through reading life writing we can get closer to the past and this in turn can enrich our understanding of our lives today.

Like other stories, life writing can take a number of forms. We can share our narratives through autobiographies or memoirs, which are first person accounts of one's own life experiences, or we can record them in diaries or journals. Life writing does not have to be about only our own life – we can write about the lives of others, too. The account of someone else's life is called a **biography**.

Writing of this variety is incredibly popular with readers and can often be found in the bestsellers section in your local bookshop. Next time you are out shopping, wander into a bookshop and take a look at how many memoirs or autobiographies are being promoted.

ACTIVITY: Life writing

■ ATL

- Collaboration skills: Listen actively to other perspectives and ideas

On your own, consider the questions below. Write down your answers on a piece of paper so that you do not forget them.

1 **Why do you think readers are attracted to real life stories?**
2 **Is it important for people to record their personal stories?**
3 **Are some personal stories more important than others?**
4 **Why should we read life writing?**
5 **Have you read any life writing? List the titles you have read and be prepared to talk about your experiences of reading these stories.**

Now get into pairs or groups of three and share your answers.

◆ Assessment opportunities

- ◆ In this activity you have practised skills that are assessed using Criterion D: Writing and Criterion C: Speaking

ACTIVITY: I Know Why the Caged Bird Sings

Maya Angelou (born Marguerite Annie Johnson) is one of the most important voices in American literature. Her remarkable life is recorded in the seven volumes of her autobiography.

- Maya Angelou

I Know Why the Caged Bird Sings is the first of these books and recounts her experiences as a child growing up in the American South in the 1930s. Through her writing not only do we get a glimpse into the inner lives of children from broken homes, but also an invaluable insight into the racial tensions which divided American society for centuries.

For years Angelou lived with her grandmother, who she refers to as 'Momma' in her writing. Read the extract on page 144 and then answer the following questions.

1. What is the relationship between the narrator, Marguerite and Bailey?
2. **Identify** two similes in the first paragraph. Choose one and **comment** on its effect.
3. How old were the children when they were sent to live with their grandmother?
4. How does Marguerite imagine California? Can you **identify** any stylistic device she uses to convey this?
5. How does the writer present a child's point of view in the extract? Think about her use of language and stylistic devices.
6. Why do the children react in the way they do after receiving their gifts?
7. What do we learn about the children's relationships with their parents? Make reference to the text in your answer.
8. What does Momma's reaction tell us about the differences in the ways boys and girls were treated at the time? Find a quote in the text to support your answer.
9. Why do you think Bailey and Marguerite 'tore the stuffing out of the doll'?
10. How does the first person narrative voice help to create more sympathy for the children?

Empathy

Imagine that you could put yourself in someone else's shoes for a short while. Well, stories allow us to do just that!

Empathy is the ability to understand and share the feelings of another person. It involves trying to see things from another person's point of view to get a better understanding of how they are feeling.

In stories, empathy can help to build a stronger connection between the readers and the characters in the story.

In pairs, **discuss** how Maya Angelou creates empathy for her characters, including her younger self, in her autobiography (see page 144).

Now, on your own, **synthesize** your ideas into a paragraph. Make sure you include evidence from the text.

One Christmas we received gifts from our mother and father who lived separately in a heaven called California, where we were told they could have all the oranges they could eat. And the sun shone all the time. I was sure that wasn't so. I couldn't believe that our mother would laugh and eat oranges in the sunshine without her children. Until that Christmas when we received the gifts I had been confident that they were both dead. I could cry anytime I wanted by picturing my mother (I didn't quite know what she looked like) lying in her coffin. Her hair which was black, was spread out on a tiny little white pillow and her body was covered with a sheet. The face was brown, like a big O, and since I couldn't fill in the features I printed M O T H E R across the O, and tears would fall down my cheeks like warm milk.

Then came that terrible Christmas with its awful presents when our father, with the vanity I was to find typical, sent his photograph. My gift from Mother was a tea set – a teapot, four cups and saucers and tiny spoons – and a doll with blue eyes and rosy cheeks and yellow hair painted on her head. I didn't know what Bailey received, but after I opened my boxes I went out to the backyard behind the chinaberry tree. The day was cold and the air was as clear as water. Frost was still on the bench but I sat down and cried. I looked up and Bailey was coming out of the outhouse, wiping his eyes. He had been crying too. I didn't know if he had also told himself they were dead and had been rudely awakened to the truth or whether he was just feeling lonely. The gifts opened the door to questions that neither of us wanted to ask. Why did they send us away? and What did we do so wrong? So wrong? Why, at three and four, did we have tags put on our arms to be sent by train alone from Long Beach, California, to Stamps, Arkansas, with only the porter to look after us? (Besides, he got off in Arizona.)

Bailey sat down beside me, and that time didn't admonish me not to cry. So I wept and he sniffed a little, but we didn't talk until Momma called us back in the house.

Momma stood in front of the tree that we had decorated with silver ropes and pretty colored balls and said, 'You children is the most ungrateful things I ever did see. You think your momma and poppa went to all the trouble to send you these nice play pretties to make you go out in the cold and cry?'

Neither of us said a word. Momma continued, 'Sister, I know you tender-hearted, but Bailey Junior, there's no reason for you to set out mewing like a pussy cat, just 'cause you got something from Vivian and Big Bailey.' When we still didn't force ourselves to answer, she asked, 'You want me to tell Santa Claus to take these things back?' A wretched feeling of being torn engulfed me. I wanted to scream, 'Yes. Tell him to take them back.' But I didn't move.

Later Bailey and I talked. He said if the things really did come from Mother maybe it meant that she was getting ready to come and get us. Maybe she had just been angry at something we had done, but was forgiving us and would send for us soon. Bailey and I tore the stuffing out of the doll the day after Christmas, but he warned me that I had to keep the tea set in good condition because any day or night she might come riding up.

Extract from I Know Why the Caged Bird Sings, *by Maya Angelou*

ACTIVITY: The story of my life

What would you include in your autobiography? Would you include everything? Or leave some things out?

Create a mind map of all the key things that have taken place in your life so far. Use the following questions help you:

● **What are your happiest memories? Which events stand out in your memory? What makes these memories so special?**
● **What have been the greatest obstacles you have faced? Was it moving to a new school? Learning a new language? How did you overcome these challenges?**
● **Who are the most important people in your life? What kind of impact have they had on you?**

Choose a particular incident in your life and write about it. Aim to write 300–400 words.

Before you begin, make a plan, using the following as a guide:
● **How will your writing start? What will happen in the middle? How will it end?**
● **Where will your writing be set? How will you establish this setting?**
● **Who will feature in your writing? (Who are the characters?)**
● **Will your writing include any dialogue?**
● **What language and stylistic choices will you make to help convey your main character's (your) thoughts and feelings?**

When you have finished, swap your writing with a partner. Highlight each other's work to **identify** examples where language and stylistic choices have been used to enrich the writing.

Give each other some constructive feedback:
● **Identify** *three* things that were done well.
● **Identify** *three* areas for improvement.

◆ Assessment opportunities

◆ In this activity you have practised skills that are assessed using Criterion D: Writing

■ ATL

■ Information literacy skills: Access information to be informed and inform others

Life writing, whether written as autobiographies or recorded in diary form, can provide us with a window into history. *Real* accounts of *real* historical events told from the point of view of *real* people can shed light on the past. Through life writing we can gain a better understanding of the way in which people lived during a particular historical period, what they thought and how they felt.

The following people are all known for keeping diaries or having written autobiographies:

• Samuel Pepys

• Anne Frank

• Olaudah Equiano

• Helen Keller

• Malala Yousafzai

In groups, find out about some of the historical events that took place during each person's lifetime. Focus on events which they recorded in their life writing.

Present your findings as a timeline.

In pairs, choose one of the people from the list above, or another person who is renowned for having produced a work of life writing. Carry out some research about them and prepare a 3–5-minute presentation for your class.

Use the following questions to help guide your research:

• Which specific text type did the writer use to convey their stories: diaries, autobiographies, letters?

• Which key historical events can we learn about through reading their life story?

• Find and read an example of their writing. This can be a short extract. What thoughts, feelings and ideas can you **identify** in their work?

• Why do you think it was important for this person to record their story in writing?

• What would you say is the message in each of their pieces of writing?

■ (Clockwise from top-left) Samuel Pepys, Anne Frank, Olaudah Equiano, Helen Keller, Malala Yousafzai

◆ Assessment opportunities

◆ In this activity you have practised skills that are assessed using Criterion C: Speaking

EXTENSION

Some of the life writers we have looked at wrote diaries.
In pairs or groups, **discuss** the following:
- Do you think the writers expected their work to be read?
- Should personal diaries be published for the public to read?
- How would you feel about someone reading your personal diary?

! Take action: How can I make a difference?

! We can all do our bit to help spread the magic that stories can bring. Here are some fun ways in which you can make a difference:

! **Set up a creative writing club at school**: Writing is a skill like any other – the more you practise, the better you get. Everyone has a story inside them waiting to break out. It does not matter if your story is a work of fiction or your life story. Put pen to paper and share it.

! **Write a biography**: Do you know someone with a really interesting life story? Immortalize them in a biography. It could be the story of one of your grandparents, a neighbour or a family friend. Biographies take a lot of research though, so start by interviewing your chosen person. You might want to record the interview using a dictaphone or on your phone (ask their permission first) so that you do not miss any of the key details. Then get writing.

! **Organize a story swap on World Book Day**: Have you read a story that you think the whole world should read, too? With the help of a teacher, set up a noticeboard in your school where you can share your recommendations. Have you got some old books lying around at home that you have already read and do not need anymore? Bring them in and swap them with someone else's books. For more ideas and to find out more about World Book Day, go to: **www.worldbookday.com**

! **Make some D.E.A.R. time**: Encourage your fellow students to read stories by asking your school to make time for reading every day – 15 minutes is more than enough. Get your teachers to set up a regular D.E.A.R. time slot (the letters stand for Drop Everything And Read) so you can all lose yourselves in a book of your choice.

SOME SUMMATIVE TASKS TO TRY

Use these tasks to apply and extend your learning in this chapter. These tasks are designed so that you can evaluate your learning at different levels of achievement in the Language acquisition criteria.

THIS TASK CAN BE USED TO EVALUATE YOUR LEARNING IN CRITERION D TO PROFICIENT LEVEL

Task 1: Write a story

- Use *one* of the images on this page as a stimulus for a short story.
- Take some time to plan your story first. You might want to **create** a mind map.
- Write 300–400 words. Remember to **organize** your writing using paragraphs.
- Follow the conventions of story writing. (Refer back to page 124 if you need to.)
- Do not use translating devices or dictionaries for this task.
- You will have 60 minutes to complete this task.

■ What will your story be about? Use one of these images for inspiration.

THIS TASK CAN BE USED TO EVALUATE YOUR LEARNING IN CRITERION B AT
PROFICIENT LEVEL

Task 2: I Capture the Castle

- Read the extract on pages 150–152 taken from the opening chapter of *I Capture the Castle* by British author Dodie Smith.
- Then answer the following questions, using your own words as much as possible.
- Refer as closely as possible to the text, **justifying** your answers and giving examples when required.
- Do not use translating devices or dictionaries for this task.
- You will have 70 minutes to complete this task.

1 **Identify** the time of day in which the narrative is set.   (strand i)
2 What is the weather like? **Identify** examples of language used to demonstrate this.   (strand i)
3 **Identify** an example in the first paragraph which suggests that the narrator is self-critical.   (strand i)
4 The family are incredibly wealthy. Is this statement true or false? Find an example from the text to **justify** your answer.   (strand i)
5 **Analyse** the effect of the narrator's use of the present tense.   (strand ii)
6 **Explain** why you think the writer switches to the past tense in paragraph 7.   (strand ii)
7 **Evaluate** the narrator's ideas about writing. Support your answer using evidence from the text.   (strand iii)
8 **Identify** which type of narrative voice has been used and **explain** its effect.   (strand i)
9 Although this is an extract from a novel, how would you describe the text type used to tell the story?   (strand ii)
10 Can you **identify** any fairy tale elements used by the writer? What might these reveal about the intended audience?   (strands i and ii)
11 How successful is the narrator in achieving the purpose she outlines in paragraph 5? **Explain** your answer with reference to the text.   (strands ii and iii)
12 **Analyse** how the narrator feels about the other members of her family.   (strand iii)
13 **Select** one of the characters from the text. **Explain** how the writer uses conventions, language and stylistic choices to establish this character.   (strand ii)
14 **Analyse** the use of humour in the text.   (strand iii)
15 The story is set in Britain in the 1930s. In your opinion, do you think that modern day teenagers from around the world would be able to relate to and empathize with the character of Cassandra, our narrator? **Explain** why or why not. Make sure you refer to the text in your answer.   (strand iii)

I write this sitting in the kitchen sink. That is, my feet are in it; the rest of me is on the draining-board, which I have padded with our dog's blanket and the tea-cosy. I can't say that I am really comfortable, and there is a depressing smell of carbolic soap, but this is the only part of the kitchen where there is any daylight left. And I have found that sitting in a place where you have never sat before can be inspiring – I wrote my very best poem while sitting on the hen-house. Though even that isn't a very good poem. I have decided my poetry is so bad that I mustn't write any more of it.

Drips from the roof are plopping into the water-butt by the back door. The view through the windows above the sink is excessively drear. Beyond the dank garden in the courtyard are the ruined walls on the edge of the moat. Beyond the moat, the boggy ploughed fields stretch to a leaden sky. I tell myself that all the rain we have had lately is good for nature, and that at any moment spring will surge on us. I try to see leaves up on the trees and the courtyard filled with sunlight. Unfortunately, the more my mind's eye sees green and gold, the more drained of all colour does the twilight seem.

It is comforting to look away from the windows and towards the kitchen fire, near which my sister Rose is ironing – though she obviously can't see properly, and it will be a pity if she scorches her only nightgown. (I have two, but one is minus its behind.) Rose looks particularly fetching by firelight because she is a pinkish gold, very light and feathery. Although I am rather used to her I know she is a beauty. She is nearly twenty-one and very bitter with life. I am seventeen, look younger, feel older. I am no beauty but I have a neatish face.

I have just remarked to Rose that our situation is really rather romantic – two girls in this strange and lonely house. She replied that she saw nothing romantic about being shut up in a crumbling ruin surrounded by a sea of mud. I must admit that our home is an unreasonable place to live in. Yet I love it. The house itself was built in the time of Charles II, but it was damaged by Cromwell. The whole of our east wall was part of the castle; there are two round towers in it. The gatehouse is intact and a stretch of the old walls at their full height joins in to the house. And Belmotte Tower, all that remains of an even older castle, still stands in its mound close by. But I won't attempt to describe our particular home fully until I can see more time ahead of me than I do now.

I am writing this journal partly to practise my newly acquired speed-writing and partly to teach myself how to write a novel – I intend to capture all our characters and put in conversations. It ought to be good for my style to dash along without much thought, as up to now my stories have been very stiff and self-conscious. The only time Father obliged me by reading one of them, he said I combined stateliness with a desperate effort to be funny. He told me to relax and let the words flow out of me.

I wish I knew of a way to make words flow out of Father. Years and years ago, he wrote a very unusual book called *Jacob Wrestling*, a mixture of fiction, philosophy and poetry. It had a great success, particularly in America, where he made a lot of money by lecturing on it, and he seemed likely to become a very important writer indeed. But he stopped writing. Mother believed this was due to something that happened when I was about five.

We were living in a small house by the sea at the time. Father had just joined us after his second American lecture tour. One afternoon when we were having tea in the garden, he had the misfortune to lose his temper with Mother very noisily just as he was about to cut a piece of cake. He brandished the cake-knife at her so menacingly that an officious neighbour jumped the garden fence to intervene and got himself knocked down. Father explained in court that killing a woman with our silver cake-knife would be a long and weary business entailing sawing her to death; and he was completely exonerated of any intention of slaying Mother. The whole case seems to have been quite ludicrous, with everyone but the neighbour being very funny. But father made the mistake of being funnier than the judge and, as there no doubt whatever that he had seriously damaged the neighbour, he was sent to prison for three months.

When he came out he was as nice a man as ever – nicer, because his temper was so much better. Apart from that, he didn't seem to be changed at all. But Rose remembers that he had already begun to get unsociable – it was then that he took a forty years' lease of the castle, which is an admirable place to be unsociable in. Once we were settled here he was supposed to begin on a new book. But time went on without anything happening and at last we realized that he had given up even trying to write – for years now, he has refused to discuss the possibility. Most of his life is spent in the gatehouse room, which is icy cold in winter as there is no fireplace; he just huddles over an oil stove. As far as we know, he does nothing but read detective novels from the village library. Miss Marcy, the librarian and schoolmistress, brings them to him. She admires him greatly and says 'the iron has entered into his soul'.

➤

Personally, I can't see how the iron could get very far into a man's soul during only three months in jail – anyway, not if the man had as much vitality as Father had; and he seemed to have plenty of it left when they let him out. But it has gone now; and his unsociability has grown almost into a disease – I often think he would prefer not even to meet his own household. All his natural gaiety has vanished. At times he puts on a false cheerfulness that embarrasses me, but usually he is either morose or irritable – I think I should prefer it if he lost his temper as he used to. Oh, poor Father, he really is very pathetic. But he might at least do a little work in the garden. I am aware that this isn't a fair portrait of him. I must capture him later.

Mother died eight years ago, from perfectly natural causes. I think she must have been a shadowy person, because I have only the vaguest memory of her and I have an excellent memory for most things. (I can remember the cake-knife incident perfectly – I hit the fallen neighbour with my little wooden spade. Father always said this got him an extra month.)

Three years ago (or is it four, I know Father's one spasm of sociability was in 1931) a stepmother was presented to us. We were surprised. She is a famous artists' model who claims to have been christened Topaz – even if this is true there is no law to make a woman stick to a name like that. She is very beautiful, with masses of hair so fair that it is almost white, and quite extraordinary pallor. She uses no make-up, not even powder. There are two paintings of her in the Tate Gallery: one by Macmorris, called 'Topaz in Jade', in which she wears a magnificent jade necklace; and one by H.J. Allardy which shows her nude on an old horsehair-covered sofa that she says was very prickly. This is called 'Composition', but as Allardy has painted her even paler than she is, 'Decomposition' would suit it better.

Extract from I Capture the Castle, *by Dodie Smith*

Reflection

In this chapter we have gained a better understanding of the **conventions** of story-writing and have explored the reasons storytellers have for sharing their work. We have also learnt that stories can be based on imagination or reality, and have explored examples of both. We have seen how writers use language and make stylistic choices to convey a certain **point of view** and in order to create **empathy** for their characters. We have applied what we have learnt in this chapter to our own writing.

Use this table to reflect on your own learning in this chapter					
Questions we asked	Answers we found	Any further questions now?			
Factual: What is a story? What are the typical conventions of storytelling?					
Conceptual: Why do we tell stories? What can we learn from stories? What makes a good story?					
Debatable: Do stories matter? Do life stories matter? What can we gain from reading personal narratives?					
Approaches to learning you used in this chapter:	Description – what new skills did you learn?	How well did you master the skills?			
		Novice	Learner	Practitioner	Expert
Creative-thinking skills					
Critical-thinking skills					
Information literacy skills					
Transfer skills					
Communication skills					
Collaboration skills					
Learner profile attribute(s)	Reflect on the importance of being open-minded for your learning in this chapter.				
Open-minded					

Glossary

abstract nouns Things which do not exist as material objects; usually ideas and concepts

acrostic poem A poem where (usually) the first letters in each line spell out a particular word or phrase

adjective A word that describes the attributes of a person, place or thing

adverb A word that describes a verb, giving more information about an action

alliteration The repetition of sounds in a sentence or a line

articles Words which determine whether a noun is specific or non-specific (the; a; an)

autobiography A first person account of one's life experiences

biography An account of someone's life written by another person

character A person in a novel, play or film

comparative adjectives Adjectives which help us to compare nouns

conjunction A word used to link together clauses or sentences

dialogue A conversation between two or more people in a story

empathy The ability to understand and share the feelings of another person

fictional Text or film describing imaginary people, events or places

first person narrative Viewpoint of a character who speaks or writes using first person pronouns such as 'I' or 'we'

genre A style of a book or film

grammar A set of language rules that help you to speak and write

idiom An expression, usually specific to a particular culture or language, which means something different from its literal meaning

imperative Verbs or sentences which are used to give commands or instructions

interjection Words or phrases that are included in speech or writing to express emotion

metaphor A literary technique which allows us to say that a person, place, animal or thing *is* something else, rather than just similar to it

multimodal texts Texts which consist of more than one mode, for instance texts which make use of both written and visual modes

narrative A story or account of events

narrator A person who tells a story

non-fictional Text or film based on true events, people or places

noun A person, place or thing

onomatopoeia Words which create or represent sounds

paragraph A series of sentences grouped together and linked by a common topic; found in prose

personification A literary technique used to give inanimate objects or concepts human characteristics

plot The main events in a novel, play or film

prepositions Words which show the relation of one noun to another

pronouns Words which can be used to replace nouns

pronunciation The way in which words or letters are said

proper noun The names of people, places or organisations; always begin with a capital letter

reporting verb A verb used to communicate what someone says, for example, say, tell, reply, ask

sentence A grammatical structure made with one or more words that can be a statement, question or command

setting The time or place in which a story takes place

simile A way of describing something by comparing it to something else, often using the word 'like' or 'as'

stylistic device Language and techniques used to create specific effects in literary and non-literary texts

superlative adjectives Adjectives used to grade nouns and say the noun is the most of that quality it could possibly be

synonym A word that means exactly or nearly the same as another word in the same language

third person narrative A story told using third person pronouns such as 'he', 'she', 'it' or 'they'

verb A word which expresses an action, occurrence or state of being

Acknowledgements

The Publishers would like to thank the following for permission to reproduce copyright material. Every effort has been made to trace all copyright holders, but if any have been inadvertently overlooked the Publishers will be pleased to make the necessary arrangements at the first opportunity.

Photo credits

p.2 © Thomas Gowanlock/123RF; **p.3** *t* © Chronicle/Alamy Stock Photo; *b* © Jean-Christophe Riou/ Age fotostock/Alamy Stock Photo; **p.9** *tl* © Ostill/123RF; *tr* © Kevin George/123RF; *bl* © Gardel Bertrand/ Hemis/Alamy Stock Photo; *br* © Joerg Hackemann/123RF; **p.10** *tl* © Alessandro Lucca/123RF; *tr* © Sean Pavone/123RF; *cl* © xxccyy/123RF; *cr* © Sborisov/123RF; *bl* © Iryna Rasko/123RF; *br* © ah_fotobox/iStock/ Thinkstock; **p.12** © National Media Museum/Laurence Stephen Lowry/DACS; **p.18** © Jeramey Lende/123RF; **p.20** *t* © datography – Fotolia, *tm* © Kybele - Fotolia.com, *bm* © Lillac - shutterstock.com, *b* © reisegraf.ch - stock.adobe.com; **p.24** *t* © EpicStockMedia/Fotolia; *b* © Elvira Rakhmanova/123RF; **p.25** *l* © ammit/123RF; *r* © mihtiander/123RF; **p.33** © Cathy Yeulet/123RF; **p.35** *l* © NejroN/123RF; *t* © jackSTAR/Cultura Creative (RF)/Alamy Stock Photo; *r* © Africa Studio/Shutterstock.com; **p.39** *t* © Wavebreak Media Ltd/123RF; *b* © Sergey Kamshylin/123RF; **p.40** *t* © JackF/iStock/Thinkstock; *c* © Mike Watson Images/Moodboard/ Thinkstock; *bl* © fuchs-photography/iStock/Thinkstock; *br* © Anetlanda/iStock/Thinkstock; **p.41** *t* © Margot Hartford/Alamy Stock Photo; *b* © BananaStock/Thinkstock; **p.44** *tl* © Trinity Mirror/Mirrorpix/Alamy Stock Photo; *c* © Jaguar/Alamy Stock Photo; *r* © Allstar Picture Library/Alamy Stock Photo; *b* © Geraint Lewis/ Alamy Stock Photo; **p.48** © Perimeter Institute; **p.50** © Dmitriy Shironosov/123RFl; **p.51** © nito500/123RF; **p.52** © delcreations/123RF; **p.55** *tl* © AfriPics.com/Alamy Stock Photo; *tc* © Pictorial Press Ltd/Alamy Stock Photo; *tr* © World History Archive/Alamy Stock Photo; *b* © Estate of Christopher Dawson; **p.56** © Igor Petrov/Shutterstock.com; **p.57** © Malachi Rempen/itchyfeetcomics.com; **p.62** © Weareteachers.com; **p.64** © Chelovek/123RF; **p.66** © designbymalex/Shutterstock.com; **p.67** © unesco.org; **p.70** *t* © AlinaMD/ iStock/Thinkstock; *l* © Anurak Pongpatimet/Shutterstock.com; *r* © Michael Blann/Digital Vision/Thinkstock; *b* © Michael Blann/Digital Vision/Thinkstock; **p.72** © Chronicle/Alamy Stock Photo; **p.76** *t* © GL Archive/ Alamy Stock Photo; *b* © Tomas Abad/Alamy Stock Photo; **p.77** © Peter Horree/Alamy Stock Photo; **p.79** © Diego Schtutman/Shutterstock.com; **p.80** © Harvepino/iStock/Thinkstock; **p.85** © World Health Organization; **p.88** © Mark Pearson/Alamy Stock Photo; **p.89** *t* © dbimages/Alamy Stock Photo; *b* © Darren Staples/Reuters/Alamy Stock Photo; **p.92** © dov makabaw/Alamy Stock Photo; **p.93** © Bill Cheyrou/Alamy Stock Photo; **p.94** *l* © Ashley Cameron/Alamy Stock Photo; *r* © Tim Graham/Alamy Stock Photo; **p.95** © Chris Jobs/Alamy Stock Photo; **p.96** *t* © s_bukley/Shutterstock.com, *b* © Keystone Pictures USA/Alamy Stock Photo; **p.97** *tl* © Pictorial Press Ltd/Alamy Stock Photo; *tr* © Mike Marsland/WireImage/Getty Images; *bl* © ROPI/Alamy Stock Photo; *br* © dpa picture alliance/Alamy Stock Photo; **p.100** *tr* © Ovidiu Hrubaru/ Shutterstock.com; *tl* © bumihills/Shutterstock.com; *cr* © LEMAIRE StTphane/Hemis/Alamy Stock Photo; *bl* © Michael Runkel/Robertharding/Alamy Stock Photo; *br* © Liba Taylor/Alamy Stock Photo; **p.101** © Boaz Rottem/Alamy Stock Photo; **p.103** Public Domain; **p.105** *tl* © Granger Historical Picture Archive/Alamy Stock Photo; *r* © Food Collection/Alamy Stock Photo; *bl* © Michal Boubin/Alamy Stock Photo; **p.107** *t* © Ant_art/ Shutterstock.com; *b* © Women Of Worth; **p.113** *t* © Sean Malyon/Cultura Creative(RF)/Alamy Stock Photo; *b* © IE186/Image Source Plus/Alamy Stock Photo; **p.120** © Soizick Meister/ImageZoo/Alamy Stock Photo; **p.122** © Ivan Kruk/123RF; **p.123** © Skylines/Shutterstock.com; **p.129** © The Granger Collection/TopFoto; **p.134** *t* © North Wind Picture Archives/Alamy Stock Photo; *b* © Lebrecht Music and Arts Photo Library/ Alamy Stock Photo; **p.135** *l* © Hilary Morgan/Alamy Stock Photo; *r* © North Wind Picture Archives/Alamy Stock Photo; **p.136** © Kablonk/Purestock/Alamy Stock Photo; **p.137** © Robertharding/Alamy Stock Photo; **p.140** © Ivy Close Images/Alamy Stock Photo; **p.141** © Granger Historical Picture Archive/Alamy Stock Photo; **p.143** © ZUMA Press, Inc./Alamy Stock Photo; **p.146** *tl* © Lebrecht Authors/Lebrecht Music and Arts Photo Library/Alamy Stock Photo; *tr* © Pictorial Press Ltd/Alamy Stock Photo; *cl* © Paul Pickard/Alamy Stock Photo; *br* © Pictorial Press Ltd/Alamy Stock Photo; *bl* © Niday Picture Library/Alamy Stock Photo; **p.148** *bl* © Pictorial Press Ltd/Alamy Stock Photo; *tc* © Angela Hampton/Bubbles Photolibrary/Alamy Stock Photo; *bc* © Angela Waye/Alamy Stock Photo; *tr* © Dave Pattison/Alamy Stock Photo; *cr* © Angelo D'Amico/Alamy Stock Photo; *br* © Brian Jackson/Alamy Stock Photo

t = top, *b* = bottom, *l* = left, *r* = right, *c* = centre

Text credits

p.19 From *Lost Cities and Vanished Civilizations* by Robert Silverberg. Used with permission from Chilton Book Publishing; **p.42** From an article by Eleanor Harding for The Daily Mail. The original article can be found at www.dailymail.co.uk/news/article-2529641/Hobbies-Wed-watch-television-Onez-four-lists-activity-favourite-pastime.html; **p.61** Excerpts from LearnEnglish Teens website. The original article can be found at http://learnenglishteens.britishcouncil.org/uk-now/read-uk/languages; **p.109** Gladwell, H. (2015). 'This anorexia sufferer became the most body confident girl on Instagram'. The original article can be found at http://metro.co.uk/2015/09/21/how-one-anorexia-sufferer-became-the-most-body-confident-girl-on-instagram-5401106/; **p.110** © Zephaniah, Benjamin (07/04/2011), *Face*, Bloomsbury Publishing Plc.; **pp.116–18** Wilson, J. (1998) *Girls under pressure*. London: Penguin Random House; **p.125** Jackson, S. (1962). *We Have Always Lived in the Castle*. New York: The Viking Press; **p.125** Golding, W. (1954) *Lord of the flies*. New York: Berkly Publishing Group; **pp.138–9** Coleman, F. (2013, June) 'Only Connect: Why Your Story Matters'. Retrieved 24 December 2016 from www.huffingtonpost.com/flynn-coleman/only-connect-why-your-story-matters_b_3492718.html; **p.144** Angelou, M. (1969) *I Know Why the Caged Bird Sings*. United Kingdom: Hachette; **p.150–2** Smith, D. (1948). *I Capture the Castle*. Boston: Little, Brown

Visible Thinking – ideas, framework, protocol and thinking routines – from Project Zero at the Harvard Graduate School of Education have been used in many of our activities. You can find out more here: www.visiblethinkingpz.org